PRE
FAB

FIRST EDITION
06 05 04 03 5 4 3

TEXT by Allison Arieff
DESIGN by Bryan Burkhart / MODERNHOUSE
Contact authors at: prefabbook@yahoo.com

COVER: "SU-SI" MOBILE HOUSING UNIT BY KFN SYSTEMS
BACK: THE TRANSPORT OF "SU-SI"
COVER PHOTOGRAPHS BY IGNACIO MARTINEZ

PUBLISHED BY
Gibbs Smith, Publisher
P.O. Box 667
Layton, Utah 84041

Orders: (800) 748-5439
www.gibbs-smith.com

PRINTED AND BOUND IN HONG KONG

Library of Congress Cataloging-in-Publication Data
Arieff, Allison.
Prefab / text by Allison Arieff; design by Bryan Burkhart.— 1st ed.
            p. cm.
Includes bibliographical references and index.
ISBN 1-58685-132-2
1. Buildings, Prefabricated. 2. Architecture, Modern—20th century.
I. Burkhart, Bryan, 1963– II. Title.
NA8480 .   A73 2002
728'.37—dc21   2002005188

PRE
FAB

TEXT BY
ALLISON ARIEFF

DESIGN BY
BRYAN BURKHART

Gibbs Smith, Publisher
Salt Lake City

A NOTE ON OUR DEFINITION of PREFAB

We admit to playing fast and loose with the concept of prefabrication here. Many of the houses presented in this book are not prefabricated in the strictest sense of the word. Not all were factory built and assembled. Some houses were built with prefabricated materials like aluminum siding. Some one-off homes were built as prototypes geared toward future mass production. In some cases, architects used prefabrication for custom homes. But all incorporate some element of prefabrication.

To my wonderful parents, Carol Arieff and Allen Arieff, for getting me my first library card, and in loving memory of my grandparents, Betty and Alex Arieff.

To my parents, Donald and Patricia Burkhart, and my gone-but-not-forgotten grandfather Francis Burkhart, who in my mind built Chicago brick by brick.

ACKNOWLEDGEMENTS

We would like to thank the numerous people who provided research assistance, read manuscript drafts, offered design advice and/or were just really nice at the right times: Adrienne Arieff, Dan Burkhart, Olivier Chételat, Taylor Haas, Patricia Hale, John Randolph, and Ann Wilson.

Many thanks to the individuals and institutions who provided indispensable archival material for this project: Julius Shulman and Judy McKee, The Arts and Crafts Society, the Chicago Historical Society, the Canadian Centre for Architecture, Central Michigan University, the Colonial Williamsburg Foundation, the Estate of R. Buckminster Fuller, the Levittown Historical Society, the Ohio Historical Society, and Archiv der Akademie der Künste.

Dwell magazine's prefab issue really helped get this book off the ground, and we would like to thank the art and editorial team for their contributions to and support of this project: Lara Hedberg Deam, Karrie Jacobs, Jeanette Hodge Abbink, Andrew Wagner, Shawn Hazen, Maren Levinson, Virginia Gardiner, Sam Grawe, Craig Bromley, and Christina Clugston. Many thanks as well to our publisher, Gibbs Smith, for approaching us to do this book, and to the staff at Gibbs Smith, Publisher, for their help in bringing it to fruition.

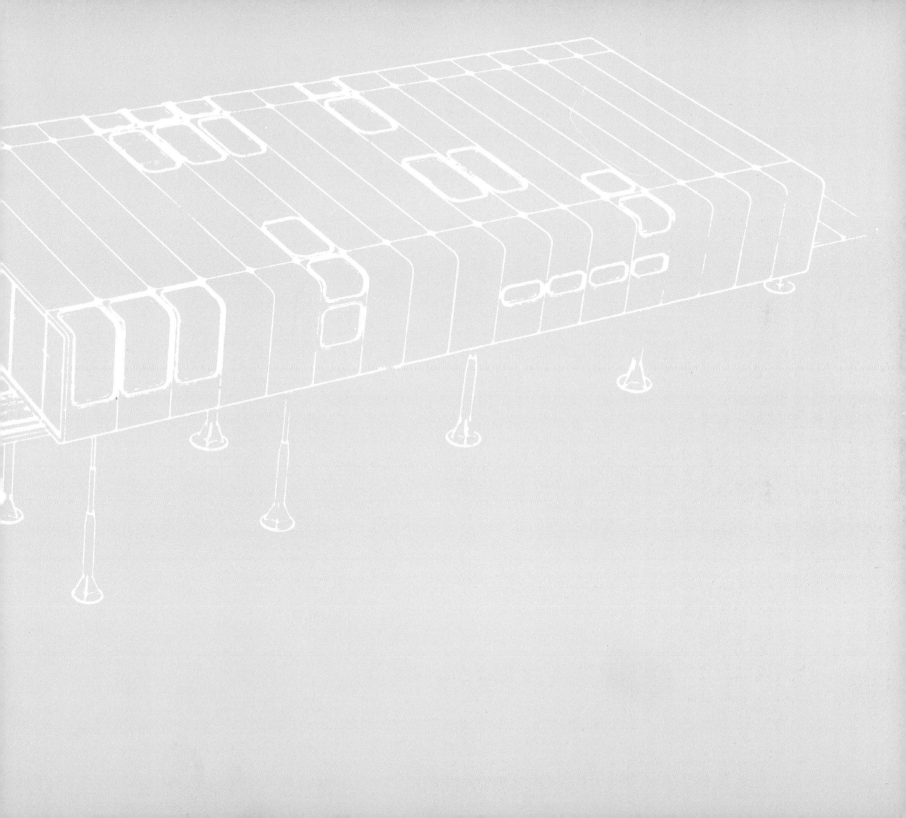

CONTENTS

134 CONCEPT

INTRODUCTION

"It can almost be taken for granted that when good prefabricated houses become a fact their architectural style will be different from the quaint English cottages and Cape Cod Colonials that are the present favorites of the speculative builders. The idea that we should take new and better building materials and mould them into the lines and textures of old materials possessing any number of shortcomings is abhorrent."

These words were spoken nearly seventy years ago by engineer Raymond Parsons at a symposium sponsored by *House and Garden* magazine in 1935. Remarkably, little has changed since then, despite wave after wave of groundbreaking proposals for prefabrication in the late thirties, again after World War II, and yet again in the late sixties from architects including Le Corbusier, Walter Gropius, Jean Prouvé, Albert Frey, Buckminster Fuller, Sir Richard Rogers, and Charles and Ray Eames.

Prefab houses have done a lot to earn their reputation for being cheap and ugly. The majority of them tend to mimic stick-built housing types like those Parsons refers to above. Others are so poorly constructed as to merit ecological designer Jay Baldwin's contention that "many prefab models are certainly CATNAP (Cheapest Available Technology Narrowly Avoiding Prosecution) and destined for early demise." Indeed, the prevailing vision of prefab associated with endless rows of charmless, cookie-cutter structures built with cheap materials and substandard construction methods is, unfortunately, fairly accurate.

There is little question that prefabrication's popularity stems from its economic benefits. The degree of control afforded by factory manufacturing, the use of standardized components, and the dramatically abbreviated construction times have helped make prefabricated housing an appealing option for many builders, developers, and home buyers. Too often, aesthetics, comfort, and quality have been sacrificed for the sake of the

bottom line. But not always. Now and throughout prefab's history, there have been many exceptions to the rule. A glimpse into the history of prefabricated housing over the last century reveals a wealth of practical and attractive alternatives to the status quo. The vision and technology exists, and has existed since the time of Parsons' lament, for prefabricated housing that is well-designed, practical, environmentally efficient, and affordable. So why isn't it being built?

Consider this: The majority of housing built in the United States and abroad is, to some degree, prefabricated, and the number of prefabricated housing units built is increasing every year. Which is to say nothing of the commercial prefab structures like Blockbuster video stores, Holiday Inn Express motels, and McDonald's franchises that have proliferated in recent decades. This development philosophy is rapidly transforming a vivid and varied landscape into a homogeneous mass lacking quality or distinction.

Most prefab buildings today are inexpensive and functional. But they need to be more than that, and, with precious few exceptions, they aren't. The reasons for this are many and varied, ranging from financial institutions' unwillingness to finance them, developers' reluctance to alter a fairly successful formula, and some architects' fears that the further proliferation of prefabrication will put them out of business. As a result of these factors and a host of others, from bad mortgages to big egos, the history of prefabrication can be seen from some perspectives as a long continuum of noble failures. The projects that have prevailed are not the most innovative or comfortable or attractive but rather are those that furnish the highest profit for developers and manufacturers.

Affordable, mass-produced housing by and large has focused on the production and assembly of the parts, as well as the construction process that then assembles the whole. Architect Peter Anderson explains that the site and the people who are to live on it "are perceived as abstract variables rather than as specific generators of form and space. In this process, modular housing systems usually reduce the assumed context and house dweller to some lowest common denominator, the assumed-to-be-most-typical site and customer." In other words, the house may be produced in the factory, but the land it is built on and the people who live in it aren't. The mistake of most producers of mass-produced housing is that they often fail to consider or acknowledge the unique factors operating when human beings and the environment are involved. That paradigm, introduced a century ago when Henry Ford's factory processes were applied to home construction, is no longer tenable.

Many doubt that prefab can ever rise above its current station. Architect, author, and builder Christopher Alexander has asserted that "the details of a building cannot be made alive when they are made from modular parts . . . modular panels tyrannize the geometry of the room." Yet we remain more optimistic. Technological advances that allow for mass customization point the way toward a new paradigm. The building type that stands poised to provide the majority of structures built in the next century has to evolve to address the needs of the individuals who will live in them. This won't happen unless all parties involved communicate—from the financier to the supplier who provides the parts to the home buyer who settles for the gable roof she did not really want.

Reflecting on a career spent trying to advance the cause of prefabrication, architect Pierre Koenig has said, "My desire was to make affordable houses for as many people as possible. I live for the day to see these houses popping out of a production line, and what a joy that would be!" By showing what can be achieved with this much maligned building type, we hope to inspire a change in the way people think of prefab and the way the architects, builders, developers, and financial institutions approach it—and ultimately, the way individuals live in it.

SILVERCREST WESTERN HOMES manufactures three houses every day. Three hundred assembly-line workers go through a million dollars' worth of materials every week. They never lose a day to weather. Photographs by Frank Schott.

ALUMINUM PANELS being constructed at the re-purposed Vultex Aircraft factory in southern California in 1946. Many aircraft companies turned to producing industrialized housing and component parts after World War II. Photograph by Julius Shulman.

A BRIEF HISTORY of PREFABRICATED HOUSING

"Eradicate from your mind any hard and fast conceptions in regard to the dwelling-house and look at the question from an objective and critical angle, and you will inevitably arrive at the "House-Machine," the mass-production house, available for everyone, incomparably healthier than the old kind (and morally so, too) and beautiful . . ."

—Le Corbusier, 1931

Prefabricated building systems can be traced as far back as the seventeenth century when a panelized wood house was shipped from England to Cape Ann in 1624 to provide housing for a fishing fleet. Swedes introduced a notched building-corner technique for the construction of log cabins just a little over a decade later. By the nineteenth century, portable structures had grown in number as new settlements and colonies were formed, and with them, a demand for immediate housing solutions. The kit houses shipped by rail during the California gold rush in 1849 are one example. Iron buildings shipped to British colonies later in the century are another. By the early part of the twentieth century, architects and inventors were experimenting with these systems for housing. In Liverpool, England, J. A. Brodie developed wood-framed duplex units in 1904. Four years later, Thomas Edison developed a poured-concrete house meant to provide workers with housing that was not only safe and affordable but also, as described by *Scientific American*, "artistic, comfortable, sanitary and not monotonously uniform." Despite Edison's best intentions, it was never built because it was simply too heavy.

By 1908, Henry Ford's Model T successfully demonstrated that mass production could be used to manufacture a high-quality object as large as a car. Factory production yielded lower prices and better quality for many consumer goods as well: the hope was that application of these production techniques to housing would similarly improve its quality, affordability, and accessibility. Industrialization was brought to prefabrication not long after Ford's Model T went into production, and by the late 1910s, a number of companies began to offer high-quality, precut, and prefabricated houses in a great variety of styles.

Aladdin Readi-Cut Houses, founded in 1906, was the first company to offer a true "kit" house composed of precut, numbered pieces. But the first and most notable company to offer houses by mail was Sears, Roebuck & Co., which sold houses through its catalogs and sales offices to nearly 100,000 clients between 1908 and 1940. Priced from $650 to $2,500, each Houses by Mail kit included lumber, nails, shingles, windows, doors, hardware, and house paint. (And instructions too, of course.) The affordable cost and ease of construction made home ownership a real possibility for blue-collar workers. It was Sears' goal to make acquiring a house as easy as buying a stove or chair. Its concept of packaging and shipping high-quality precut materials and precise instructions directly to the buyer was sound. The volume of homes sold allowed Sears to maintain flexibility and offer its clientele a wide variety of designs. Its skillful marketing strategy convinced thousands of Americans that a Sears house would offer them the comfort and security of their dreams.

Desperate for new housing after the devastation of World War I, European countries embraced prefabrication as a time- and cost-effective method of building. Britain, France, and Germany were developing prefabricated systems of concrete and steel while Sweden focused on wood systems. Perhaps the most architecturally significant of these early European developments in prefabrication came from the French architect Le Corbusier. His 1914 Dom-Ino House had a new type of skeletal-framework construction of reinforced concrete that formed the floors, supports, and stairs of a building and eliminated the need for load-bearing walls.

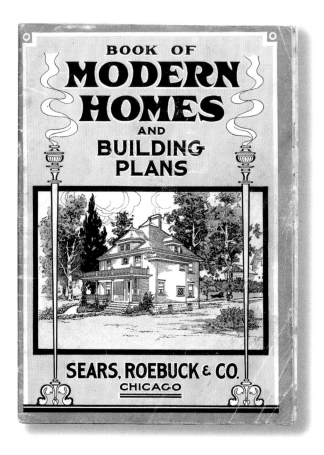

ALADDIN HOUSES Based in the booming lumber town of Bay City, Michigan, Aladdin was the first company to offer a true kit house with precut numbered pieces. The company enthusiastically promoted the high quality of its wood, offering customers $1 for every knot they found. The company sold approximately 65,000 Readi-Cut model homes before going out of business in 1981. Catalog cover courtesy of the Clarke Library, Central Michigan University.

HOUSES BY MAIL Sears, Roebuck & Co. of Chicago sold about 100,000 mail-order kit houses from 1908 to 1940. Catalogs featured a selection of models that the buyer could customize to his own specifications. Sears' goal was to make ordering a home as simple as ordering any other household product. Catalog cover courtesy of Rob Schweitzer and The Arts & Crafts Society.

Le Corbusier developed a number of mass-produced housing schemes and was a fervent advocate of the genre, as articulated in his spirited essay "Mass Production Houses," written in 1919: "If we eliminate from our hearts and minds all dead concepts in regard to the house, and look at the question from a critical and objective point of view, we shall arrive at the 'House-Machine,' the mass-production house, healthy (and morally so too) and beautiful in the same way that the working tools and instruments which accompany our existence are also beautiful." The architect's enthusiasm was limitless, but regrettably he produced little beyond some theory on his utopian ideals and on his modular building scale. Le Corbusier was instrumental, however, in the development of the International Style of architecture that would influence modern buildings over the next several decades.

Walter Gropius, founder of the Bauhaus, had called for the industrialization of housing as early as 1910. Indeed, its development was one of the main goals of the Bauhaus effort to create "a new architecture for a new age." In 1923, working with Adolf Meyer, Gropius developed "Building Blocks," a system of standardized flat-roofed housing. Three years later, he designed a construction system for a housing estate at Toerten-Dessau. There was no shortage of architects and engineers interested in exploring the possibilities of steel during this period. Muche & Paulick, Carl Kaestner Company, the Woehr Brothers, and Bruane and Roth all developed steel-house prototypes in 1926.

These early experiments had yet to reach American shores, however, because the work of European modernists like Le Corbusier, Gropius, Mies van der Rohe, Alvar Aalto, and JJP Oud was not familiar to most Americans. But when the Museum of Modern Art in New York presented its first architectural exhibition in 1932, *The International Style: Architecture Since 1922,* the European modernists were introduced to the United States. The philosophy and style of this esteemed group of modernists would exert tremendous influence on U.S. architects. The International Style did not have a major impact on home building in its American infancy, but its impact on the course of architecture over the next thirty years was immeasurable.

Sears, Aladdin, and other similar companies in the United States were enjoying moderate success with the sales of their kit houses and saw no reason to embrace the industrial aesthetic of the Internationalists. They didn't have to. Prefabrication was steadily making its way into the larger popular consciousness and culture. Buster Keaton, for example, starred in a short film about building a prefab house. In *One Week* (1921), Buster and his new bride proudly set about the business of building their dream house—a prefab with puzzling instructions.

Builders and architects were clearly interested in the promise of mass-produced houses and experimented with various materials and technologies. In 1927, Robert Tappan introduced a steel-framed house and Buckminster Fuller introduced his design for what would later become the Dymaxion House. Still, the prefabricated housing industry was slow to expand. It took the depression in 1929 to generate a real interest in mass-produced housing in the United States. The impetus for that interest was the hope that housing starts would help stimulate the lagging economy.

The housing industry had followed the model of the automobile industry in order to develop factory processes for construction; and further, the depression had fostered a climate in which factory-built homes seemed the only practical option. Archibald MacLeish declared in a 1932 issue of *Fortune* magazine that "It is now past argument that the low-cost house of the future will be manufactured in whole, or in parts, in central factories, and assembled on the site. In other words, it will be produced the same way as the automobile." [1]

The economic climate led Howard T. Fisher to develop the General Houses Corporation in 1932. This new company would act as an assembler of parts ordered to its own specifications that would then be produced by building-component suppliers (companies on board included General Electric, the Pittsburgh Plate Glass Company, and Pullman Car and Manufacturing). Seen as the General Motors of the housing industry, General Houses produced affordable homes ranging in price from about $3,000 to $4,500. The company's first house was built for Fisher's sister-in-law in 1929. General Houses went on to produce a number of model homes made from pressed steel based on standardized parts designed by Fisher, who was optimistic about the public's taste for contemporary advances in housing. [2] "The final decision in the matter of design will of course depend on what the public wants," he explained at a symposium sponsored by *House and Garden* in 1935. "But in everything else the

1. H. WARD JANDL. *YESTERDAY'S HOUSES OF TOMORROW: INNOVATIVE AMERICAN HOMES, 1850–1950.* THE PRESERVATION PRESS, NATIONAL TRUST FOR HISTORIC PRESERVATION, 1991, p. 72.

2. ALLAN D. WALLIS. *WHEEL ESTATE: THE RISE AND DECLINE OF MOBILE HOMES.* NEW YORK: OXFORD UNIVERSITY PRESS, 1991, p. 135.

HOUSE OF TOMORROW George Fred Keck's three-story, twelve-sided house built in 1933 had glass walls and an airplane hangar but no takers. Photograph by Hedrich-Blessig, courtesy of the Chicago Historical Society.

public has shown a preference for the best in modern design, and I doubt it will pay extra for fake imitations of the past when they buy their houses." Fisher's predictions about public taste would ultimately prove to be off the mark—Americans just weren't ready for houses straight off the assembly line. But before that became apparent, other companies—including American Homes, American Houses, Inc., and the Homosote Company—optimistically followed his lead.

Steel was increasingly becoming an integral part of the housing industry in the thirties. Several steel producers were backing research on its use for prefabrication. A number of steel-prototype houses generated from that research were presented at the Chicago World's Fair in 1933. Builder George Fred Keck's House of Tomorrow and Crystal House were both displayed at the fair's Century of Progress Exhibition. Each exhibition house was supported by a steel framework and steel-deck floor system. A standout at the exhibition, Keck's House of Tomorrow was an eye-catching, three-story, twelve-sided structure built on a steel frame. It featured glass walls and even an airplane hangar (complete with a small

Curtiss-Wright sport biplane inside) on its ground floor. The house had central heating, air conditioning, and window-shading devices to control the level of incoming light. Keck took advantage of the cost savings from the house's prefabricated elements and applied them to quality-of-life features such as large outdoor decks, frosted glass walls in the bathroom, a built-in aquarium in the children's room, and the latest technological innovations in the kitchen. More than 750,000 people toured the House of Tomorrow in the first year of its exhibition. No commissions were forthcoming, but the house's popularity did enable Keck to build a second house for the exhibition, even more radical than the first.

Keck's Crystal House had an innovative prefabricated structural frame that was erected in just three days, but its bold constructivist aesthetic was a bit too radical for the average home buyer. That, combined with its less-than-prime location on the fairgrounds, got in the way of its success. The house was sold for scrap at the end of the season; its materials and furnishings were auctioned off by Keck to pay the bills. A Chicago real-

MOTOHOME Small two-story, flat-roofed International Style houses, like this one built in 1933, were advertised as the "prefabricated houses that come complete with food in the kitchen." Courtesy of the Canadian Centre for Architecture, Montreal.

WICHITA HOUSE Buckminster Fuller was interested in creating affordable and efficient housing solutions. Mass production was a move in the right direction but the public wasn't quite ready for a round house. Courtesy, The Estate of R. Buckminster Fuller.

estate developer purchased the House of Tomorrow along with six other fair houses. The group was then loaded onto a barge and transported to Beverly Shores, Indiana. Keck and his younger brother William continued to build prefabricated houses, including some that made use of passive solar concepts.

Robert McLaughlin of American Houses, Inc., like many of his architectural colleagues, saw economic opportunity in the field of low-cost housing. After unveiling a prototype in 1932, McLaughlin introduced his own brand of prefabricated houses known as American Motohomes. The steel-framed houses ranged from a six-bedroom, four-bathroom, two-car-garage model to a simple four-room home. Each house, promised McLaughlin, possessed "durability, beauty, economy, and convenience to a degree the world has never known before." The components were fabricated in a factory in New Jersey and then assembled on-site. The turnkey houses even came "complete with food in the kitchen." The flat-roofed, geometric residences that subtly referenced the International Style did not have the mass appeal that McLaughlin had anticipated,

however, and American Houses, Inc., abandoned the Motohome for more conventional prefabricated home building.[3]

Despite the struggles architects and builders were having with their more innovative housing concepts, a number of independent thinkers were intrigued by the potential of prefabrication and were eager to put their ideas out there. Visionary thinker, engineer, architect, and designer Buckminster Fuller had begun investigating mass-produced housing in 1927 with the goal of providing "efficiency in living." He focused his efforts on designing homes that would have mass appeal and yet be practical both for the buyer and for the environment. Fuller had the technology licked, but his inability to accurately gauge public taste continually thwarted his attempts at actually producing the houses he designed.

Fuller's earliest concept for what would come to be known as the Dymaxion House was first presented to the public in 1929 when G. Ray Schaeffer, the promotions manager of Marshall Field's department store in Chicago, asked Fuller to design a house that would showcase the store's furniture to increase its customer appeal. Fuller called his house "4-D" but the store wanted something a little catchier. Schaeffer called in Waldo Warren—a marketer famous for coining the word "radio" to take the place of wireless—to come up with a new name. Warren spent two days listening to Fuller talk, and after taking copious notes on Fuller's rant, he combined three of Fuller's favorite words—dynamic, maximum, and tension—to come up with the unique name Dymaxion. Hexagonal in shape and held together using tension suspension from a central mast, the structure was a far cry from any conventional home and handily demonstrated Fuller's exhortation to "do more with less." The house had a living/dining room, two bedrooms, two bathrooms, a library, and even a sundeck on the roof. It could be easily disassembled, transported, and reassembled, reflecting Fuller's desire to create efficient shelter for better living.

Fuller's Dymaxion prototype got a lot of press but not a lot of takers. The world might be ready for the Dymaxion House, suggested a 1932 headline in the *New Orleans Tribune*, "When We Live in Circles and Eat in Merry Go-Rounds." Fuller experimented with other Dymaxion designs, including a bathroom (a single unit holding a tub, toilet and sink, sliding doors, and heated metal surfaces) and a car (three-wheeled and fuel-efficient but unsafe at many speeds), but it would be another twenty years before Fuller saw his design built.

Viennese émigré cum California modernist Richard Neutra was also experimenting with prefabrication around this time. (He would even install prefabricated bathrooms in the very high-end Windshield House in 1938.) Neutra's Lovell Health House, built as a demonstration house in 1928–29, had a lightweight prefabricated steel frame, and his Hollyridge Estate, built in 1932, utilized standardized wood-chassis construction. Neutra's personal architectural philosophy, what he called "biorealism," emphasized man's relationship to nature and seamlessly merged prefabricated building materials like steel frames and glass with a natural aesthetic. Neutra's colleague and fellow Austrian Rudolph Schindler focused less on prefabrication than Neutra, but his use of concrete, flat roofs, and clerestories profoundly influenced the course of California modernism—a movement that would become intimately linked with the dream of innovative, affordable housing.

Albert Frey, a Swiss architect who had worked for Le Corbusier in Paris before moving to America in 1930, made his contribution to the prefab discourse with the Aluminaire. Conceived with his partner, architect A. Lawrence Kocher, the Aluminaire bore the distinct influence of Le Corbusier's work from the 1920s. Described by the architects as "A House for Contemporary Life," the project was presented at the Allied Arts and Building Products Exhibition in 1931. Borrowing a bit from the General Houses model, Frey and Kocher solicited suppliers—including the Aluminum Company of America, the McClintic-Marshall Corporation (a subsidiary of Bethlehem Steel), and Westinghouse—to donate materials so the house could actually be constructed for the exhibition. It became the first all-light-steel-and-aluminum house built in America. The prototype was purchased at the 1931 exhibition by architect Wallace K. Harrison and rebuilt on Harrison's property on Long Island. Frey and Kocher experimented with other prefabricated housing types, including two prototype farmhouses, an Experimental Five-Room House, and an Experimental Weekend House. These innovative explorations with materials like steel, aluminum, and canvas no doubt contributed to the development of Frey's singular aesthetic, which, due to the lack of substantial developer and consumer interest, were never realized.

Another independent spirit, architect Frank Lloyd Wright also took on the challenge of creating a well-designed, affordable house. When potential clients Herbert and Katherine Jacobs arrived at his studio at Taliesin in 1936 with a proposition to design "a decent five-thousand-dollar house," he gladly accepted, telling his new customers that he'd wanted to design a low-cost house for years but that no one had ever asked. And so, the first Usonian House was designed and built. Wright was inspired rather than hindered by the cost restrictions. The "obstacle" made the process more interesting. "The house of moderate cost is not only America's major architectural problem but the problem most difficult for her major architects," Wright told *Architectural Forum* in 1938. "As for me, I would rather solve it with satisfaction to myself and Usonia, than to build anything I can think of at the moment."

For his Usonian houses, Wright had developed not a prefabricated system per se but rather a grid system that established regular, modular dimensions for the wooden houses. This grid allowed for maximum design flexibility and also unified the group of buildings. Each design, however, was unique. The repetition of standard details reduced costs, as did the elimination of items considered standard for most other single-family homes. The features deemed unnecessary included a visible roof, a garage (a carport was provided), a basement, and roof gutters. More radical in their absence were radiators, light fixtures, furniture, bric-a-brac, paint, and plaster. People living in a Wright house had to accept quirks along with his genius. They wore sweaters in the winter and learned to live with built-in furniture. Approximately two dozen more Usonian houses were designed between the mid-thirties and early forties.

Universities, art museums, and the rare adventurous client may have been ready to accept the innovative concepts of visionaries like Fuller, Wright, and Gropius, but the average consumer wasn't there yet—even for the decidedly less radical houses of builders McLaughlin and Keck. The conventional housing industry's primary goal in the thirties was to simply make residential design and construction more practical and, by extension, more inexpensive. And home buyers didn't seem too troubled by that business decision.

The impact of modernism espoused by many of the architects and risk-taking developers was minimal. Builders of apartment buildings in the thirties went right on putting Tudor or French provincial details on their brick façades. Most houses built in the thirties were largely built by hand, woven together from plaster, lath, brick, and other materials. The new building materials like aluminum, enamel, or steel, along with methods of prefabrication introduced in the same decade, finally were used primarily to make the traditional methods of building cheaper and more automatic. In 1942, the General Panel Corporation had commissioned architects Walter Gropius and Konrad Wachsmann, who had both immigrated to the U.S. from Germany during the war, to design a system of standardized

"Prefabrication is all things to all men, and a source of confusion to many. . . . Its basis is not so much a logical theory as a cult. And as a cult it has won ardent and persuasive adherents, united by a belief in a better house, for less money, through more efficient methods of house production."

—Bruce and Sandbank, *A History of Prefabrication*, 1944

GENERAL PANEL HOUSES In the 1940s and 1950s both avant-garde architects and mass-market homebuilders were interested in new technologies and techniques of production. An example is the prefabricated "Packaged House" (later known as the General Panel House) developed by Walter Gropius and Konrad Wachsmann for the General Panel Corporation in 1942. Courtesy of Konrad Wachsmann Archive, Archiv der Akademie der Künste.

panels. The architects applied their system to a General Panel House but the project never left the boards. General Panel Corporation continued to develop structures using General Panel components. Other systems like the prefabricated panel developed by Howard T. Fisher also facilitated functionality and low cost, but most of the houses utilizing these systems tended to be boxlike, with none or few of the planning innovations advocated by early-twentieth-century modernists.

It is not wholly surprising that design innovation was not a major concern at a time when housing of any sort was desperately required. Government agencies stepped in to help improve the housing situation with new legislation and agencies like the Farm Security Administration. Established in 1937, the FSA made a concerted effort to inform the public about mass-produced housing, a program that included the sponsoring of several low-cost-housing demonstrations around the country. In FSA's second year, it built 1,000 homes for sharecroppers in Missouri, using prefabricated walls and roof sections. In 1939, the agency built fifty steel-framed dwellings at a cost of $1,650 each. Other federal agencies did their part to develop the industry as well, but the growth of the prefabricated housing market was slow. Between 1935 and 1940, prefabricated homes accounted for about 10,000 homes, or just less than one percent of the nation's total production for that period. By 1940, there were only thirty firms manufacturing this sort of house. A new infusion of government support after the war would soon help to stimulate that growth significantly. Further, trailer homes were slowly gaining in popularity during this period, though financing of these ostensibly portable homes remained problematic.[4]

Approximately 18,000 prefabricated homes had been built by the end of 1941. Several federal agencies had been contracted for or had built roughly 1.6 million housing units during the war, of which over 12 percent had been prefabricated. The housing crisis continued to be so dire that President Harry Truman appointed Wilson Wyatt as Housing Expediter in 1946 to help stimulate the production of housing for veterans returning

QUONSET HUTS

The Quonset hut was developed at the beginning of World War II by engineers Peter Dejongh and Otto Brandenberger of the George A. Fuller Construction Company (no relation to Buckminster). After the Navy had contacted them about developing inexpensive, portable shelters, Dejongh and Brandenberger set up a production facility near Quonset Point, Rhode Island, and began producing units while their design was still being fine-tuned. Icons of military presence, Quonset huts were designed as prefabricated shelters that could be easily shipped anywhere in the world and readily assembled by untrained troops in the field. The Quonset's arched form was strong and lightweight, composed of a ribbed metal shell with wood-framed end walls. The semi-cylindrical form was copied from the British Nissen hut, though its construction differed considerably. Principal improvements over the Nissen type included an interior pressed-wood lining, insulation, and a tongue-and-groove wood floor. More than 170,000 Quonset huts were produced during World War II, and many of these rugged structures still survive today in new lives as shops, warehouses, stores, and housing. Quonset huts were mostly put to use as industrial buildings, churches, and student and emergency housing, though a few notable exceptions are the glowing Quonset-hut home and studio that French architect Pierre Chareau designed for painter Robert Motherwell in the Hamptons in 1947, and architect Bruce Goff's modernist chapel in Camp Parks, California, in 1945. (Above, *Saturday Evening Post* illustration of a Quonset designed by Roy M. Franceski for the Hires Bottling Company in Lodi, California, 1948.)

WORKERS AT THE VULTEX AIRCRAFT COMPANY demonstrate the strength of one of the aluminum panels used in an affordable house prototype designed by architect Ed Larrabee Barnes and industrial designer Henry Dreyfus in 1946. Photograph by Julius Shulman.

from the war as part of the Veterans' Emergency Housing Program. Prefabricated housing played a large part in Wyatt's proposal to Truman. "The Expediter" hoped to have a quarter of a million prefab units under construction in 1946 and an additional 600,000 the following year. "We can meet this need only by bringing to bear the same daring, determined and hard hitting team work with which we tackled the emergency job of building the world's most powerful war machine four years ago," Wyatt stressed in a 1946 report to President Truman. The promise of federal support to prefabrication builders significantly helped to stimulate growth in the industry. Their number nearly tripled—up to 280 in 1946 from just 100 the year prior.

And their brand of experimental design got a bit of a boost in 1939 when the New York World's Fair proclaimed the supremacy of the Modern. As Russell Lynes recalled in his 1949 book, *The Tastemakers*, one witnessed, "a city of geometrical shapes, of Trylon and Perisphere, of strip windows and ramps and flat roofs and glass walls." Like the White City of the Columbian Exposition of 1893, which had celebrated the triumph of the Beaux-Arts, the New York World's Fair announced in indisputable terms that Modern of a sort was here to stay—at least for awhile, and at least so far as industrial building was concerned. Lynes argued that the Second World War was instrumental in advancing the cause of modern design, at least for awhile. "People were glad to live in anything," he writes, "even Quonset huts."

Recognizing the housing shortage as a window of opportunity, Buckminster Fuller reintroduced his Dymaxion concept during the war. Presented to the United States military as the awkwardly monikered "Airbarac Dymaxion Dwelling Machine," this housing complex was designed to easily accommodate officers' housing, barracks, and a four-deck hospital ward. Fuller designed a structure to be built from aluminum, which was, at the time, the alloy developed for warplane construction. Despite its many advantages, the government rejected Fuller's idea due to a lack of the necessary building materials.

Meanwhile, in Kansas, the Beech Aircraft Company needed housing in order to keep a rapidly dispersing workforce from seeking employment in other industries. The company saw the Dymaxion Dwelling Machine as a good option. Fuller's small, lightweight house was inexpensive, easy to maintain, and built to withstand Kansas tornadoes. But its unconventional round shape, coupled with labor disputes and Fuller's refusal to comply with his investors' guidelines, caused the project to fall apart. One prototype house was built in Kansas.

Fuller's continuing fascination with housing systems that were compact and transportable continued. In 1948, he gave his students at the Institute of Design in Chicago the task of designing a "Standard of Living Package," a container, transportable by trailer, that could hold complete furnishings for a household of six. And later that year, he would develop his first geodesic structures. In 1949, Fuller presented his design for the Wichita House, which consisted of lightweight standardized aluminum units that were to be assembled at the site. Republic Aircraft was set to produce it. Though the well-publicized house drew over 30,000 expressions of interest from around the country, Republic, in the end, manufactured only two.

To make up for the decline in aircraft manufacturing after the war, many aircraft companies attempted to adapt their factories and technology for home manufacturing. Vultex Aircraft commissioned industrial designer Henry Dreyfus to do a prototype affordable house for production. Designed in collaboration with architect Ed Larrabee Barnes, the walls of the Dreyfus house consisted of single full-sized panels made from paper cores skinned with aluminum. Manufactured off-site, these panels were to be transported to the desired location and then erected. The project was funded by the federal government's Guarantee Market program, created to provide housing and employment for workers making the transition to a postwar economy. Several other aircraft companies were developing prototype homes in an effort to make up for the decline in airplane manufacturing after the war, but none ever went into production.

In 1948, the Lustron Corporation began producing prefabricated, all-steel houses in a surplus wartime aircraft factory that had been used to build Curtiss-Wright fighter planes. The idea for a prefabricated, all-steel dwelling wasn't new, but Lustron founder Carl Strandlund was initially more adept at marketing it than his predecessors. "This is the house America is talking about," color advertisements for Lustron proclaimed—and America was.

THE LUSTRON CORPORATION began producing prefabricated enameled steel houses in 1948 but bad management helped bring the company to an early demise. Courtesy of the Ohio Historical Society.

SPARTAN AIRCRAFT COMPANY Spartan advertisements like this one were designed with the house trailer population in mind. At $5,000 each, they cost a bit more than the average Levittown house.

Strandlund excelled at making friends in Washington at a time when government funding was essential to house building. In 1947, his company received a $15.5 million loan from the government, the post–World War II equivalent of venture capital. Strandlund was great at publicity and influence peddling but he wasn't as good at closing a sale or balancing the books. Though the choice of house colors was novel (as was the idea of hanging pictures on the walls inside with magnets), consumers weren't entirely convinced, and though the price was low, it wasn't low enough. An even more serious obstacle was that more than 3,000 parts totaling over twelve tons of steel were needed for each house, and despite the tremendous interest generated in its product, the company could never really afford to produce it. Approximately 2,500 Lustron houses were built before the company folded in 1950. (Its demise may also be partially attributable to some questionable business practices, including a $10,000 fee the company paid to Senator Joseph McCarthy for his essay "A Dollar's Worth of Housing for Every Dollar Spent." Strandlund had also been bankrolling McCarthy's gambling outings at the racetrack.)

Spartan Aircraft Company went in a different direction and began to manufacture house trailers rather than conventional houses. Incorporating the structural technology of the airplane, the Tulsa, Oklahoma-based company

manufactured house trailers that were constructed from aluminum sheets riveted to a ribcage-like frame (the "monocoque" design was first developed by William Hawley Bowlus in the early thirties). First manufactured in 1947, the Spartan trailer was the first trailer expressly designed as a house. Spartan enjoyed considerable success with its category-defying shelter. Unlike prefabricators and merchant builders whose projects were dependent on subsidized mortgage programs, Spartan's combination of mobility, affordability, and availability allowed the company to thrive.[5] Perhaps an alliance would have suited both parties, but for the most part, advocates of industrialized housing ignored the trailer industry.

Throughout the industrialized world, individuals continued to push the boundaries of industrial production in architecture. In Australia, for example, architect Harry Seidler was commissioned to design a prototype industrialized production house that was later built in conjunction with the Royal Australian Institute of Architects Convention in 1954. Constructed from locally available materials, the prefabricated sections, columns, and open web beams could be erected by four men in just one day. The house was displayed at Sydney Town Hall for the duration of the convention but was never actually built. Seidler's goal was extreme flexibility. Nearly any floor plan could be constructed with

HARRY SEIDLER The Australian architect's low-slung prototype reveals the influence of his instructor Walter Gropius, who he studied with at Harvard. Photograph courtesy of Harry Seidler & Associates.

LEVITTOWN helped facilitate the American Dream of home ownership after World War II. Photograph courtesy of the Levittown Historical Society.

a system of panels he developed, in contrast to the "monotonous sameness" (as Seidler put it) of typical prefab houses. The house also featured a prefabricated bathroom. The mechanical parts of the kitchen and the laundry room were also conceived of as one-piece packaged units. Seidler had been a student of Walter Gropius at Harvard, and his work was clearly influenced by his teacher's belief in the need for more economical (both in terms of cost and scale) housing.

In France, furniture designer Jean Prouvé was similarly concerned with avoiding the repetition and monotony characteristic of most mass-produced housing communities. When commissioned by the French government in 1950 to design a mass-produced housing scheme, Prouvé developed a plan that called for fourteen variations of two design types. Twenty-five units were built and installed in Meudon, France. For this group of houses, Prouvé had developed a jointed steel structure that could be erected without scaffolding—a technique that he had used on numerous occasions, most notably with his frequent collaborators Pierre Jeanneret and Charlotte Perriand, for housing, hospitals, and other buildings. Like many early prefab experiments, the Meudon houses, perhaps because of their modern aesthetic, were sold to the fairly well-off rather than the lower-income population for whom they were intended.

Prouvé had successfully demonstrated that the houses could be produced on a large scale, but the French government chose not to adopt his design and no additional homes were produced.

Companies like Butler Steel Products, ARCON, and Alcoa were making further advances in systems for steel and aluminum housing, largely inspired by a desire to adapt to the new postwar economy. Thanks in part to these newly developed systems, builders and developers were able to undertake vast housing projects by the 1950s. A government-guaranteed financing program that had been established in 1944 under the auspices of the Veterans Administration mortgage program also facilitated this expansion. This new program was far more effective than Wilson Wyatt's, which had suffered greatly with the defeat of the Democrats in 1946. With the incentives of the guaranteed-mortgage program, housing starts jumped from 937,000 in 1946 to 1,692,000 in 1950. Though prefabricated housing builders often had difficulty obtaining these mortgages (a problem that continues to the present day) and had lost a powerful ally in Wyatt, several companies ventured into the rapidly expanding housing industry with varying degrees of success. In addition, the Housing Act of 1949 was passed in continuing recognition of the national and pervasive housing crisis following World War II.

PIERRE KOENIG'S STAHL HOUSE (CASE STUDY HOUSE #22) epitomized the ideals of modern domestic life at mid-century. Photograph by Julius Shulman.

"The American residence is becoming a product and eventually all homes—except those of the very wealthy—will be bought in prefabricated form."

—Craig Ellwood, 1957

Developer William Levitt was very adept at making the new government legislation work for him. Levitt, inspired by Ford, pioneered mass-produced construction techniques that helped the housing industry meet the overwhelming demand. This was due in large part to the size of Levitt's operation. The more houses built, the lower the overall cost. Further, Levitt brought the factory to the site, where workers poured foundations, erected frames, installed plumbing, and so forth. Even more crucial to his success, Levitt focused not on individual homes on individual sites but on an entire housing community. In 1945, Levitt began developing Levittown, Pennsylvania, and by 1948 he was putting up 150 houses a week. He continued at that pace until 6,000 were completed. Filling an entire subdivision with Levitt-built homes allowed him to assure all prospective home buyers that their homes were eligible for FHA or VA financing.

For better or worse, Levitt's brand of community development would set the standard for future housing systems. The typical Levittown house in 1950 had an entrance foyer, a living room with log-burning fireplace, two bedrooms, a kitchen with a General Electric refrigerator and electric range, a bathroom, and a porch or carport. Other features included copper radiant heating, aluminum venetian blinds, insulated glass, and a built-in TV. Looking like so many ants on a hill, these massive clusters of standardized houses seemed outright depressing, but these neighborhoods of mass-produced houses did not deter most aspiring homeowners. In 1953, a writer in *Harper's* observed that all that exterior sameness was not a problem, as the standardized house appeared to have created "an emphasis on interior decorating. Most people try hard to achieve something different. In hundreds of houses, I never saw two interiors that matched—and I saw my first tiger-striped wallpaper."

In 1949, developer Joseph Eichler, Levitt's West Coast counterpart and founder of Eichler Homes, Inc., considered such repetition unacceptable. Levitt's standardized houses used 2 x 4 construction, while Eichler utilized post-and-beam construction to create his new modern homes. Most builders typically didn't hire architects to design houses, but Eichler did. He wanted to make money, of course, but he was also intent on designing houses of the highest quality. Like Levitt, Eichler focused on acquiring entire subdivisions, but his decisions incorporated more quality-of-life aspects such as green space and cul-de-sacs to reduce traffic. Eichler houses had other innovative features like an open plan, glass walls (including an airy inner atrium, which would become the hallmark of Eichler homes), and a second bathroom at a time when most homes had only one. Once Eichler Homes made the second bath a standard feature, other builders had to follow suit. Influenced by Frank Lloyd Wright and California modernists including Richard Neutra, Eichler houses embraced the California landscape, and their architecture emphasized the relationship between inside and out. Young first-time buyers were drawn to the modern lifestyle that Eichler Homes promised.

In 1945, a housing program was introduced that became the standard by which all other attempts at well-designed, affordable single-family homes were measured. Like many of the housing schemes initiated after the war, the Case Study Houses program was fueled by the rising demand for affordable single-family homes and the need to house a generation of GIs returning from the war. But unlike every other housing program, the Case Study program was launched not by a builder, developer, or even an architect, but by John Entenza, the enigmatic editor of *Arts and Architecture* magazine. Entenza's vision provided an extraordinary opportunity for a generation of American and émigré architects to pursue an unprecedented experiment in modern domestic architecture. Over the course of twenty years, thirty-six Case Study Houses were designed and built, each intended as a model for future construction on a mass scale. Architects such as Edward Killingsworth, Charles and Ray Eames, Richard Neutra, Raphael Soriano, Craig Ellwood, and Pierre Koenig proved they could build cost-effective homes without compromising modernism's utopian principles.

EICHLER COMMUNITIES were a pleasant alternative to William Levitt's sprawling developments.

MOBILE HOMES were promoted as the answer to America's dire postwar housing shortages but failed to deliver the domestic bliss its proponents promised.

The husband-and-wife team of Charles and Ray Eames designed one of the first Case Study Houses for themselves. The colorful, airy home and studio located in the hills of Pacific Palisades openly celebrated its steel-frame structure and came to symbolize the California modernist lifestyle. Architect Craig Ellwood designed three Case Study Houses—Nos. 16, 17, and 18—between 1952 and 1958. All three were low-slung, flat-roofed, single-story structures of steel and glass. The former engineer's appreciation of prefabricated technologies inspired him to leave the houses' steel frames exposed. "The increasing cost of labor and the growing lack of craftsmen—our expanding machine economy—will more and more force construction into the factory where units will be manufactured for fast job assembly," he explained to *Progressive Architecture* in 1959. Pierre Koenig also used steel-frame structures and industrial technology to generate his own architectural style. His work always stressed the importance of the natural expression of materials rather than gratuitous ornamentation. Koenig, who designed Case Study Houses 21 and 22 (the Bailey House and the Stahl House, respectively), has said that the failure of these houses to be put into production caused him deep regret.

Reflecting on photographer Julius Shulman's enduring images of these now-iconic houses, writer Luc Sante has observed, "They were the offspring of the marriage of European theory with the free-spending and limitless southern California landscape. They had aristocratic veins and factory workers' hand, tons of cool mathematical rigor and no fancy stuff. They knew their kind would soon be everywhere, the way big cars and Scotch highballs were everywhere. Then the earth revolved a few times. Economic cycles passed, and so did their moment."

Indeed, it was not the sleek Case Study prototypes that took off but the more generic planned-community paradigm—this despite the fact that such developments were somewhat disreputable. A popular novel of the period, John Keats' *A Crack in the Picture Window* (1956), condensed all the potential horrors of the planned community into one cheap paperback that, despite its lowbrow form, referenced real complaints and social trends, from divorce to unpaved roads, that were surfacing during the postwar years.

The problems associated with planned communities probably paled in comparison to the assumed tawdriness of mobile-home parks that were opening at a rapid rate. This expansion was due in part to the introduction in 1954 of Marshfield Homes' "Ten-Wide," a mobile home that was two feet wider than the conventional eight-foot model common to the industry. Marshfield's Ten-Wide was popular because of the extra space and privacy it afforded, but it caused tremendous upheaval. It took up more room in the factory, which created production problems, as well as on the highway, leading many states to restrict its mobility. It ultimately forced the hand of trailer manufacturers, who had to choose between producing narrower models (recreational vehicles) or the wider ones (mobile homes). By 1963, these two industries split.

Mobile homes were typically designed to look like either trailers or permanent homes, but a third aesthetic emerged briefly around the time the Ten-

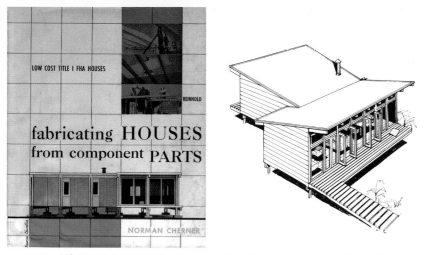

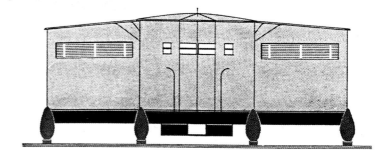

NORMAN CHERNER embraced prefabrication and espoused a do-it-yourself approach to it in his book (above), which was published in 1957 with the subtitle "How To Build a House for $6,000." One of the architect and furniture designer's plans is shown above.

MOBILE HOMES

In 1936, designer William Bushnell Stout forecasted (and enthusiastically awaited) the Age of the Mobile Home. His version, seen above—a mobile metal house that could be folded, towed by car to a location and then pulled open into something three times the size of a trailer—was ingenious. But the housing industry saw it as a trailer, not a house, and at $2,600, Stout's sleek shelter couldn't compete in the marketplace. The mobile home has been unable to shake its less-than-illustrious reputation, but that hasn't stopped it from having its share of proponents. Perhaps the most ardent advocate of this disparaged building form was architect Paul Rudolph who, in the late sixties, proclaimed it to be "the twentieth century brick." Rudolph's prediction was pretty much off the mark, but there have been a number of designers and architects who have experimented with the mobile home in an attempt to remove the stigma that seems to be attached with super glue. In the 1980s, Deborah Berke designed a modular-house concept, known as Single Wide, Double Wide, that would have allowed home buyers to order the model they selected—ranging from a basic 1,800-square-foot "double wide" to a sprawling (well, it was still considered sprawling in the eighties) 3,500-square-foot ranch house—and then have it delivered to their chosen site where it would be installed per their specifications. The firm of Duany Plater Zyberg also endeavored to enhance the reputation of the lowly form with their Rosa Vista Mobile Home Park, designed in 1992. The New Urbanist architects began by creating walkways along the center of extra-wide blocks and a pedestrian network free of cars. While the potential of the mobile home park has yet to be realized, it continues to be a source of fascination for architects intrigued by the idea of creating likeminded communities from well-sited, well-designed structures. (Image of Stout's mobile house courtesy of Milton Newman.)

Wide was introduced. A small group of companies aiming to capitalize on the increasing popularity of industrial design promoted the mobile home as an industrial product. Raymond Loewy—who had designed everything from the Avanti automobile to the logo for Lucky Strike cigarettes—was hired to develop a new line of mobile homes in the mid-fifties. In 1963, the Marlette Company commissioned an industrial-design firm in Chicago to develop prototypes that bore a striking resemblance to Mies van der Rohe's sleek modernist boxes. (The company reverted back to its more conventional styles within a year.) Even Frank Lloyd Wright's designs were tapped. National Homes commissioned Wright's Taliesin Studio to design a "Prairie-style" mobile home. The final version was used for display purposes but never built. The low cost of mobile homes attracted buyers more concerned with shelter than style, which helps to explain why the higher-end versions failed to go into production. The mobile-home industry quickly got over its infatuation with modernism and committed itself to the fetching "rectangular" vernacular. By 1960, homes on wheels would account for 15 percent of the nation's housing dollar, amounting to fully one-quarter of all single-family homes by 1968.

Prefabricated, mobile, and manufactured housing companies proliferated in the fifties, and their goals were focused far more on financing than design. Fleetwood, which started off as a recreational-vehicle company, began creating "homes away from home" for an American public fascinated by their new ability to travel the United States by automobile, and went on to expand their scope to manufactured housing. As the market for

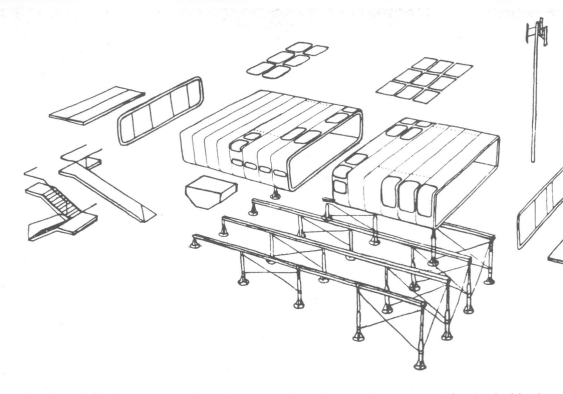

RICHARD ROGERS The futuristic Zip-Up program made use of monocoque construction and demonstrated the architect's interest in sustainable and prefabricated technologies. Rogers saw the concept as rooted in do-it-yourself principles and envisioned potential purchasers going to their local building supply store to customize their own version of it. Diagram courtesy of Richard Rogers Partnership.

housing stabilized, buyers were less desperate and could demand more freedom of choice and better quality. Prefab homebuilders suffered from those increased customer expectations as a result. The rapid-fire construction that had taken place after the war resulted in many homes of substandard quality, and now the prefab industry had to answer for it. The industry looked for ways to enhance its maligned product. By developing new techniques, even new descriptive terms for their products, many companies attempted to distance themselves from prefabrication altogether.

Carl Koch, the founder of Techbuilt, developed a housing system that took advantage of prefab technology without sacrificing individuality. Eager to distance his product from the prevailing stigma of prefab, Koch stressed that the Techbuilt home was not a package, "but a system of converging components that the builder and owner complete at their discretion." Though it may have been a matter of semantics, Koch's wording was a savvy move and helped Techbuilt achieve a great deal of success in the fifties and sixties. Other emerging companies believed that houses produced wholly or partly by machines didn't need to look industrial (modern), and the resulting model homes offered were typically Tudor, Colonial, Cape Cod, or ranch style. These more traditional vernacular types

set the standard for the majority of the factory-built homes by companies like Silvercrest, Fleetwood, and Kaufman and Broad that followed.

As new challenges faced housing in the sixties and seventies, architects developed new concepts to confront them. In Britain in the sixties, many of the country's most innovative architects devoted themselves to the task of creating affordable, well-designed mass housing that addressed emerging social concerns from the fight for civil rights to solutions to the energy crisis. Architect Sir Richard Rogers developed the Zip-Up Enclosures in 1968, a series of inexpensive, low-maintenance shelters that offered a high degree of environmental control and a large range of design choices. The Zip-Up system of construction utilized a snug-seam joint from Alcoa and could be built in a matter of weeks using existing standard components. The home's lack of internal structure allowed maximum flexibility for partitions—demountable components run on retractable castors—and allowed the house to be extended out or up by adding or removing panels.

Rogers later developed a concept for an Autonomous House that would function as an artificial ecosystem, recycling its own water and waste, heating or cooling itself using natural energy, and generating its own

DOMES

Around A.D. 100, Roman builders rotated an arch in a circle and discovered that it created a strong three-dimensional shape—and the monolithic dome was born. In time, churches and mosques were topped with this new and brilliant design. Essentially a three-dimensional arch, the dome is a curved structure without corners or angles. Domes can enclose an enormous amount of space without the help of a single column or other support. Despite their thin skins, domes are exceptionally strong and durable. The form, however, never took off as a widely accepted residential building type. Today domes are most commonly used for commercial structures like exhibition centers and stadiums (though in 2000, a computer company did make plans to build an entire city in India composed of 4,000 monolithic domes to house its engineering employees). Buckminster Fuller's geodesic versions, like his 1967 Expo Dome seen above, are the most distinctive manifestations of the form. (Courtesy, The Estate of R. Buckminster Fuller.)

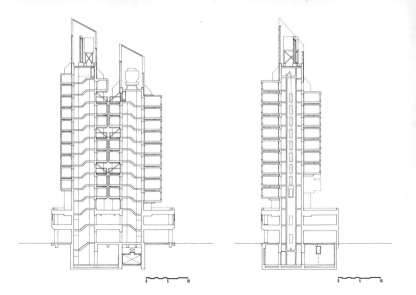

power. The Autonomous House, which looked as if it was about to make a lunar landing, stood on adjustable legs that raised it above the ground and rested on strip footings that provided stability and minimized the building's impact on the site. "Man can change his lifestyle and home to conform to nature and therefore curb his traditional destruction of the natural world," Rogers explained in the project brief. "His activities can then merge into the ecological system and his architecture can become complementary, rather than parasitic toward natural resources."

Britain's wildly eccentric Archigram Group created fantastical urban scenarios that addressed a plethora of contemporary issues from traffic to overpopulation. Their creative, often outlandish concepts for "capsule" apartments, "Walking Cities," "Instant Cities," and "Plug-In Cities," strongly influenced their contemporaries in Japan, Europe, and the United States. While many of these other architects were working on similar concepts, Archigram was unique in its ability to distill processes and ideas and disseminate them to a wider public. The eccentric collective responded energetically to the culture around them, and their work embraced everything from moon landings to the Beatles. Archigram's members never meant for their radical creations to be built, only to inspire, provoke, and entertain.

In the States, new housing systems took advantage of advances in science and technology from solar panels to space stations and applied them to shelter. Ray Kappe's Advanced Technology House was com-

NAKAGIN CAPSULE TOWER Completed in 1972, this was the world's first capsule architecture built for actual use. Kisho Kurokawa's tower was meant to draw residents from the suburbs back to central Tokyo, and was designed to accomodate the changing needs of residents. Photograph and drawings, opposite, courtesy of Kisho Kurokawa.

ADVANCED TECHNOLOGY HOUSING
Architect Ray Kappe wanted to create an energy-efficient, transportable module (right) that could be controlled by computer. Drawing courtesy of Ray Kappe.

missioned by NASA in the sixties with a primary goal of demonstrating technology transfer to housing. Integral to the Advanced Technology House was the concept of a modular unit that was usable in various horizontal and vertical configurations, transportable, adaptable to different climates and site limitations, and energy efficient. Kappe proposed a glass skin that could change from clear to opaque and provide insulation, and a power unit that could be disengaged to provide personal transportation, ideas that significantly influenced subsequent explorations into sustainable technology and modular building systems.

Buckminster Fuller remained hard at work on unique dwellings, too. Back in 1954, he had patented the icosahedron (a twenty-sided polyhedron with each side made up of an equilateral triangle) principle, and by the early sixties, he began to build structures based on that principle. Fuller touted these structures, known as geodesic domes, as a breakthrough in building technology and firmly believed in their potential for mass production. Intrigued, the U.S. Information Agency commissioned Fuller to design the U.S. Pavilion at the World Expo in Montreal in 1967. Fuller presented the Expo Dome, a geodesic three-quarter sphere with a diameter of seventy-six meters and a height of sixty-one meters. "If industry was to take it on, there are things we could do in geodesic domes that are spectacular," Fuller wrote in 1971. But domes seemed to be favored by hippies and naturalists for the freedom and flexibility they promised. The building industry was far less enthusiastic. Though Fuller's geodesic dome was considered by many to be his masterpiece, the

form never gained the acceptance he had hoped for. (However, the "Buckminsterfullerene" family of molecules based on Fuller's geodesic structure that was discovered by scientists Kroto, Smalley, and Curl in 1985 did help that trio win the Nobel Prize in 1997.)

Fuller's Expo Dome wasn't the only curious structure at the Montreal Expo. Also on display was Moshie Safdie's Habitat Montreal. Safdie was only twenty-four at the time and had never built anything before. His concept for the experimental housing scheme was deceptively simple. One hundred fifty-eight houses were constructed from 354 modular units. Eighteen different types were created based on the single box measuring 17.5 x 38.5 x 10.5 feet. The "houses" were built one on top of the other so that the roof of one formed the garden of the next. Each concrete module was a standard-sized living unit with an individual roof terrace. But the construction and fabrication were far more complex than Safdie's design suggested. Poured concrete was simply too heavy a material for the design. The finished structure was safe but the process of constructing it had been quite dangerous. This, combined with the cost of using custom production-line tools and molds rather than standard-issue ones, sent the project into a budgetary stratosphere—$22 million, which was almost double the amount originally allotted. "I'm convinced," Safdie observed in his book, *Beyond Habitat*, published in 1970, "that no one is going to be able to mass produce a house until the entire process is under a single corporate structure, and probably a single union, too. Yet factory-made and produced housing

RAMOT HOUSING COMPLEX Architect Zvi Hecker's 720-unit "beehive" (at left), erected in 1974 in Jerusalem, was influenced by capsule architecture but utilized polyhedric rather than rectilinear modules. Photograph by Michael I. Schiller.

is the magic word being whispered as the key to salvation. Present practice," he continued, "is impossible."

British architect Paul Rudolph learned from some of Safdie's missteps. He believed that Safdie's choice of building material was the problem, not the experimental nature of the design. In 1968, Rudolph addressed (at least on paper) the "weight" problem that had vexed Habitat in a commission for the Amalgamated Lithographers of America, a building that was to accommodate 4,050 prefabricated residential units built on 65 floors, with 13 floors of industrial space for the lithographers and printers, plazas, traffic-free streets, and parking for 2,100 cars. This was a dream project for Rudolph; better still, the lithographers were not deterred by his $280 million estimate. He was thrilled by the promise of prefabrication. "When we first started seriously to think about the prefabricated home, everybody jumped to the conclusion that it would lead to monotony. I say it offers us a way of building truly imaginative and exciting homes." Rudolph's dream building was scrapped, however, when it faced opposition from other unions and from local government. In 1971, Rudolph went on to design many prefab structures, including a modular housing complex known as Oriental Masonic Gardens in New Haven, Connecticut. Local building codes got in the way of the cost-effectiveness of Rudolph's modular scheme; he had more success with corporate buildings like the Daiei Headquarters building in Nagoya, Japan, commissioned by a real-estate developer who built and sold prefabricated houses.

Japan became a fulcrum for innovative prefabrication in the sixties, most notably from the work of architect Kisho Kurokawa, who had his own particular brand of prefab known as "capsule architecture." Kurokawa's Nakagin Capsule Tower (1970) was an inner-city project that aimed to create sustainable living space in the heart of Tokyo. Straight from the space age, the Nakagin Capsule Tower was the architect's most successful realization of his volumetric architecture concepts. Contemporaries of Kurokawa—including Warren Chalk of the Archigram Group, who had begun using the word "capsule" in 1964—were also exploring the notion of capsule architecture at this time, but the Nakagin tower was the world's first capsule architecture built for actual use. The scheme provided for the eventual replacement or removal of capsules over time, depending on the spatial needs of the tenants. The connection of units, for example, could transform a studio apartment into a two-bedroom unit to accommodate a growing family. "By creating spaces of autonomy and individual identity, this building symbolizes individual human existence in the urban landscape," Kurosawa explains. "This is symbiosis between material and spirit." Kurokawa saw a lot of potential in volumetric architecture. This flexibility applied to factory-manufactured components pointed the way toward a shift in prefab's practical applications. Kurokawa factored in the individual's needs within a standardized framework.

Israeli architect Zvi Hecker was equally fascinated with the stacking of components but opted to dispense with rectilinear forms altogether

SHIPPING CONTAINERS

Like heavy Legos for grown-ups, shipping containers made of steel or aluminum can be used as an inexpensive basic "building block" for a variety of facilities and housing. Containers are stronger than an average, conventionally built residence and can be used for either temporary or permanent structures. Easily transported by ship, train, or truck, containers are watertight, designed to withstand incredible stresses in shipping, and are resistant to such forces as hurricanes, tornadoes, and earthquakes. Containers are easily expandable and can take on a variety of appearances with the addition of new materials to existing façades. Engineer Richard Martin founded Global Peace Containers, a not-for-profit organization that has perfected a system to convert retired containers into housing and community buildings for third-world countries. Wes Jones Partners used standard shipping containers as the basic module for construction for their "Technological Cabins" in the High Sierras (above). The New York–based partnership LOT/EK has created several container-based structures including the conceptual Mobile Dwelling Unit (MDU), which is designed to travel with its owner/inhabitant from one long-term destination to another. The transportable live/work space would be able to plug into towers located around the world to obtain power, water, sewage lines, and networking capabilities. Built shipping container developments already exist in Oakland, California, and are planned elsewhere in cities like Rotterdam, Holland. And in 2001, Australian architect Sean Godsell developed Future Shack, a stylish and functional emergency housing prototype built from a discarded shipping container. If the mobile home was "the twentieth-century brick," as Paul Rudolph once proclaimed, the shipping container may well be taking its place in the twenty-first. (Rendering courtesy of Wes Jones Partners.)

when he designed the Ramot Housing Complex in Jerusalem in 1974. Polyhedric modules were used to form a cluster of 720 units, also known as the beehive. In Germany, the firm of Hübner-Forster-Hübner also developed a variation on the theme with octagonal capsules made of plastic rather than steel for their Casanova House built in 1975. Twenty-three prefabricated cells were installed in a cluster on the site of a former dump located just outside Stuttgart. Each unit was delivered to the site fully equipped with wiring, heating, plumbing, and even wallpaper and carpeting.

Inspired by technological advances and challenged by social and economic realities, architects continued to push the boundaries of not just prefabricated houses but the idea of housing itself. Domes, yurts, earthships, and other unconventional (and prefabricated) structures had their moment but remained at the margins. Few discernible changes were made with regard to the design and manufacture of prefabricated housing in the latter part of the twentieth century. But there are rumblings of some positive transformations as the twenty-first century gets started. Established home builders like Lindal Cedar Homes, and Acorn and Deck Houses, for example, have endeavored to expand the range of plans, materials, and vernacular styles available within their repertoire. Young architects and architecture students worldwide continue to be fascinated with the promise of well-designed, affordable housing, as their experiments with virtual, sustainable, mobile, and/or temporary shelters attest. Even designers of custom homes are recognizing the environmental and economic benefits of prefabricated systems. Although industrial designer Ron Arad is better known for his innovative chairs, tables, and modular storage units made from industrial materials like injection-molded plastic and aluminum, for example, he made use of boat-building technology to develop radical new forms and off-site prefabrication for his one-off Amiga House designed in 1999.

Ideally, prefabrication combines traditional materials with contemporary aesthetics to create innovative housing solutions. In truth, the majority of new housing constructs—prefab and stick-built alike—cling to a formula that fails to address the evolving nature of families, the need for energy efficiency and environmental sensitivity, and a more modern vernacular style desired by a new generation of home buyers. The homes we are used to have less and less relevance to our contemporary needs. It is imperative that the home evolves to meet those needs.

Architect Wes Jones has observed, "The contemporary vernacular is the product of a speculative, real-estate developer consumerism which is self-consciously but unwittingly devolving into a kitsch-pastiche of formerly legitimate postures toward dwelling. The unconsciousness and ubiquity that makes this a vernacular does not reflect the traditional pervasive concern for efficiency and attendant sense of appropriateness, but a market-driven vision of what that should be, as capricious as the consumer pool and the advertising dollars which stir it." Jones's points are salient but as his explorations into new modular systems have demonstrated, we should not abandon hope just yet. Prefabrication for the twenty-first century allows for repetition of the same systems without replication of the same house, and this promise of mass customization may be the last best hope for prefab that really works.

In a lecture in 1929, Buckminster Fuller was asked what prefabrication meant for architects. Didn't he see, one observer asked, that the mass production of houses might very well make the architect obsolete? Fuller disagreed. "The architect's efforts today are spent in the gratification of the individual client," he responded. "His efforts of tomorrow, like those of the composer, the designer of fabrics, silver, glass and whatnot may be expanded for the enjoyment of vast numbers of unseen clients. Industrial production of housing, as contrasted with the present industrial production of raw materials and miscellaneous accessories, calls for more skill and a higher development of the design element, not its cessation."

Fuller was right on the mark. There are today a host of architects and designers who continue to be compelled to explore the possibilities of technologies currently available as well as those yet to be discovered. Hopefully, their work will help to alter the prevailing perception of prefab as low quality and poor design, and it is their work—in production (or poised to be), custom-built, and conceptual—that follows.

THE FUTURE OF PREFAB? The innovative use of prefabrication combined with good design holds great promise for housing in the future.
(Above) Prefab house frame by Johannes Kaufmann and Oskar Leo Kaufmann. Photograph by Ignacio Martinez.

PRODUCTION

A diverse group of well-designed houses and multi-family

dwellings that are either in production, or poised to be.

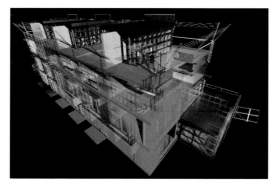

PHOTOGRAPHS BY STUDIO MARKKU ALATALO

"Touch" House

Heikkinen Komonen Architects
Location: Helsinki, Finland

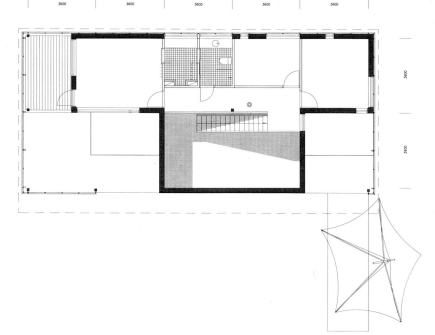

Known as "Touch," this single-family house by the Finnish architectural firm of Heikkinen Komonen was designed for mass production and is made from large prefabricated units that are assembled and surface-finished at the factory. The "Touch" prototype, originally commissioned by the building company, Kannustalo Ltd., was well received at the Tuusula Housing Fair in Finland where it was first exhibited in 2000.

Though over 90 percent of single-family houses in Finland are prefabricated, most are traditional in their design, looking to historical pastiche rather than contemporary aesthetics. Heikkinen Komonen's goal was to make a different, more modern option for young families. The firm was also interested in creating a design suitable for both urban and suburban environments. The resulting house has a conventional exterior shape that belies

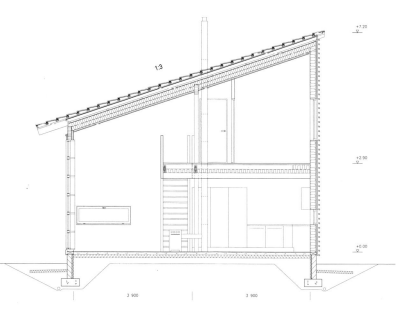

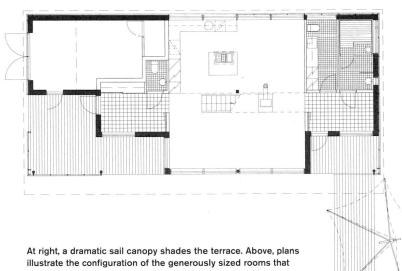

At right, a dramatic sail canopy shades the terrace. Above, plans illustrate the configuration of the generously sized rooms that are grouped around a 1-1/2-story open "farmhouse" living area. Furnishings divide the living, kitchen, and dining areas into separate zones within a unified area of varying heights.

The level of detail found in this striking single-family house is atypical of factory-built housing. The tiled roof has glazed portions over the veranda, balcony, and sauna terrace that bring light into the middle of the house. The front entrance is shown on the opposite page, lower left.

the variety of forms found internally. "The house has a simple, contained character from the outside," explains architect Mikko Heikkinen, "but inside is spatially rich and full of light." The challenge was to make this happen within the dictates of what factory manufacturing can accommodate.

This was a challenge met. The unique character and attention to finishes and detail are atypical, given the house's factory-made origins. This is a firm that seems to transform obstacles into advantages with ease as its diverse projects—ranging from a sleek cylindrical headquarters building for McDonald's in Helsinki, Finland, to a villa made from stabilized earth in Guinea—attest.

The house's mono-pitch roof forms a foursquare compact envelope around a series of varied outdoor spaces. Glazed portions of the house's tiled roof that hang over the veranda, bedroom balcony, and sauna terrace bring natural light into the middle of the building's frame. All rooms are grouped around a one-and-a-half-story, open living/dining/kitchen area. Furnishings help divide these zones within a unified area of varying heights.

Since their introduction, two "Touch" houses have been put into production, and the company has received queries from around the world, from New Zealand to Korea to New York. The Kannustalo factory is equipped to make ten houses per year.

 PHOTOGRAPHS BY ÓLAFUR MATHIESEN

Summer House
Gláma Kím Arkitektar
Location: Hálsasveit, Iceland

In Iceland, building a vacation house in town and moving it to the site is more the rule than the exception. Why? Simple. That's where the labor is. Prefabricated construction is quite common in the country as a means to an end. So when Ólafur Mathiesen of Gláma Kím Arkitektar in Reykjavík began to conceive of a summerhouse for a family of five in Hálsasveit, approximately two hours northwest of Reykjavík, a prefabricated structure was the logical choice.

Mathiesen designed a straightforward, two-volume structure comprised of a main house, measuring 4 x 13 meters, that contains an open kitchen/living/dining space, entryway, bathroom, and exterior storage space, as well as a small structure measuring 4 x 0 meters that contains the sleeping areas. The two are connected by a glazed walkway. A small veranda connects to a sauna and hot tub, positioned to the north. The house is heated by geothermal water from wells located on the property. Living areas open up towards the south and west while a distant view to the northeast looks out to Hálsasveit's nearby Strutur Mountain and the glacier Eiriksjökull.

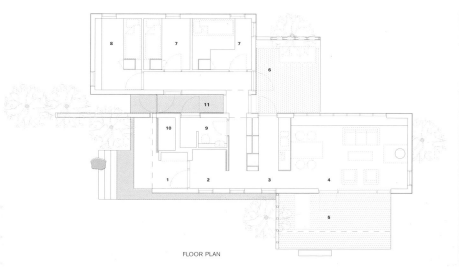

FLOOR PLAN

The house consists of two rectangular volumes. Both are wood frame clad in corrugated steel. Inside, walls and floors were done in birch plywood. No space or materials were wasted. All storage spaces are built-in and furnishings are minimal.

The larger building was trucked to the location (above and right) and then hoisted into place. The dimensions of the structure were dictated by the size of the truck bed. The smaller building was built in parts and erected on-site.

The larger of the home's two units was erected off-site, transported to the location, and hoisted into place. Its size was dictated by the limitations of transportation (the size of the truck bed and the access road to the property). The smaller building was built in parts and erected on-site. Both structures are wood frame with cork parquet flooring. The exteriors are clad in corrugated steel (specifically Alu-zinc), the interiors in birch plywood. Cupboards and shelves are built-in and furniture is minimal. Corrugated metal is a common feature of the agrarian, urban, and industrial vernacular of Iceland. Its longevity and ease of maintenance has only increased this material's popularity in recent years.

The owners, a professional couple with three children, wanted a place that would provide a significant contrast to their full-time city dwelling. The architect fulfilled this desire by creating a simple but striking home that takes maximum advantage of the spectacular view surrounding it. The use of readily available materials combined with the ease of construction and simplicity of design make this home ideally suited to mass production.

The elegantly spare design allows the landscape to take center stage. That combined with its use of simple, affordable materials makes the Summer House an ideal prototype for prefabricated vacation homes.

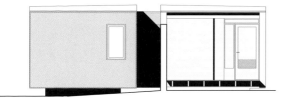

NORTH

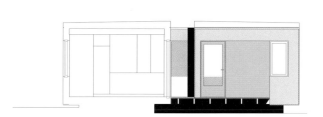

SECTION THROUGH MORNING VERANDA

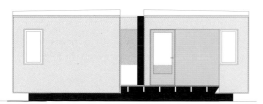

SOUTH

EAST

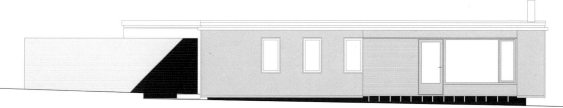

WEST

PHOTOGRAPHS BY STAFFAN JOHANSSON

Bo Klok ("Live Smart")

IKEA (in cooperation with Skanska Bostäder)
Locations: throughout Sweden

Bo Klok ("Live Smart"), the prefabricated housing program developed by IKEA in collaboration with the Swedish building company Skanska Bostäder, doesn't pack flat but it is, like the company's furniture, comfortable, affordable, and well-designed. Early on, Skanska and IKEA recognized that a prefabricated unit would be the most cost-effective housing program to undertake. The use of prefabricated elements allowed a new apartment block to be constructed in a period of only six weeks. This standardization of construction, design, and materials makes it possible for these apartments to be offered at incredibly reasonable prices: each one-bedroom Bo Klok apartment rents for about 3,000 SEK (approximately $300 U.S.).

The first Bo Klok apartment concept was designed to create the most livable environment possible while keeping costs low. Before proceeding with the Bo Klok concept, IKEA took the often-ignored step of asking potential tenants what they wanted from their housing. The answers were fairly consistent: a safe environment, a garden, light and space, natural materials, good functionality, and storage space. And, of course, good value for their money.

The company paid close attention to the desires of its market, and the resulting scheme, Bo Klok—the literal translation is "live sensibly"—is practical and affordable, with an eye to good design on a human scale. Each two-story building has just six apartments, with not more than thirty-six apartments per site. These smaller-scale developments help to prevent the complexes from looking like housing projects. In truth, the basic efficiency of Bo Klok's exteriors are somewhat reminiscent of dormitories or army barracks, though the color scheme and limited number of developments help to curtail that effect. The sensitivity to the surrounding landscape reflected in the way the buildings are sited is another plus.

In a country that sees so little of it for most of the year, light is of paramount importance. In response, all Bo Klok apartments take in light from three

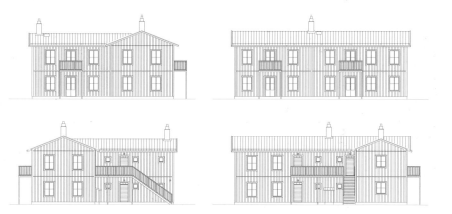

An example of Bo Klok (opposite page) in Malmö, Sweden, where IKEA is headquartered. The simple exteriors are slightly reminiscent of barns or barracks but the interior spaces have high-quality finishes and lots of windows. The open kitchen (above) has oak floors and is outfitted with IKEA components like these birch cabinets. The quartet of drawings illustrate the variety of Bo Klok configurations available. Each complex is built to the particular requirements of its site.

Before the design phase began, potential tenants were asked what they wanted from their living space. The resulting amenities are intended to enhance the tenants' quality of life. In addition to convenient locations and affordable rents, each unit has its own washing machine, parking space, storage area, and garden.

perspectives. All units have a private garden area, high ceilings, and a washing machine. Upon move-in, each resident is given a gift of two free hours with an IKEA personal interior designer as well as a voucher for new IKEA furniture (plus two hours labor from a technician who will put it all together). Kitchens eschew the particle board and linoleum characteristic of conventional prefabs and opt for birch cabinetry, oak flooring, and extra-high windows. And in contrast to the paper-thin ceilings one would expect, the company developed an acoustic ceiling (an environmentally conscious solution made primarily of recycled glass) to address their findings that one-third of the residents were dissatisfied with the sound environment in their homes.

The first Bo Klok house was built in Ödåkra, near Helsingborg, in 1996. Bo Klok units have since been constructed throughout Sweden in cities and towns, including Stockholm and Älmhult (where IKEA was founded). Though the design focus is clean and modern, there are regional taste variations that dictate exterior finishes and materials. A minimum of a thousand additional Bo Klok apartments is planned for Sweden in the early 2000s. The concept is also being exported to other countries, including England, Norway, Denmark, and Poland. "It's clear," explains Anders Larsson, product manager of Bo Klok, "that we have developed a form of living which has aroused great interest everywhere."

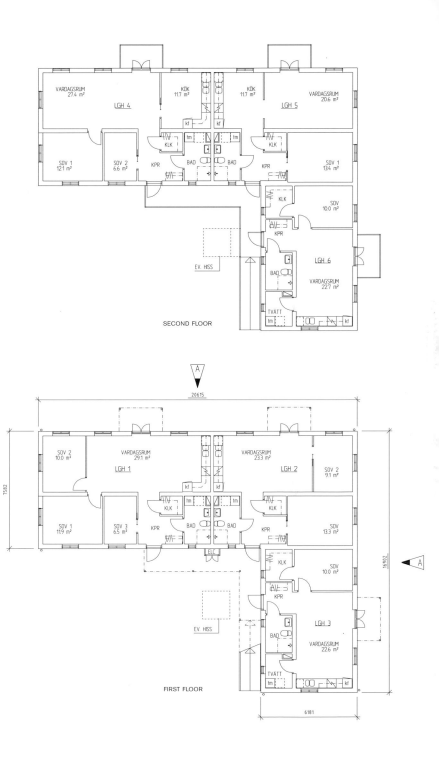

PHOTOGRAPHS BY JULIO PEREIRA

The LV Home
Rocio Romero
Location: Laguna Verde, Chile

For just $30,000, designer Rocio Romero designed and built this informal yet elegant vacation home for her parents in Chile. The considerations of how her family would interact in and around the house was a major component to Romero's design. But the family played an even more central role when construction began and Romero shared contracting duties with her mother, Soledad Valdes. "With my architectural experience and my mother's experience with construction in Chile," Romero explains, "we knew that we would make a good team. And since we did all of the general contracting for the project, we ended up saving a lot of money, of course."

The sleek and minimal weekend retreat is located in Laguna Verde, a small town south of Valparaiso, Chile. Romero's design goal was to create an inexpensive, compact, functional, low-maintenance home with a relaxed and elegant atmosphere. She credits Mies van der Rohe for inspiring the design for this and "almost every project I've designed. Modern architecture just doesn't get much better than what he has already done." Lush Laguna Verde was another major inspiration for Romero's project. "I don't think there is a more stunning coast than the Chilean coast, and the landscape in Laguna Verde is just unbelievable. It was so clear for me that this vacation home had to be all about having the exterior become the interior landscape."

The LV Home's elongated plan, high ceilings, and continuous northern sliding-door façade give every main room a completely seamless view of the beach. The wood frame-and-metal structure sits on concrete piers. The exterior of the 970-square-foot house is primarily corrugated zincalume, aluminum, laminated glass, and concrete, while the interior is a combination of drywall and stained plywood. The two bedrooms and the living/dining area line the northern side of the home, and the bathrooms, kitchen, laundry, and closets are tucked in the back along the southern side of the home. "I was interested in developing a prototype for a mass-producible home," Romero explains, "so simple, straightforward gestures as well as dimensions that made it easy for the house to be trucked to the site were the constraints I imposed on the home."

Mies van der Rohe, and his Farnsworth House in particular, is a clear influence on Romero's work. The Venice, California–based designer also embraces the indoor/outdoor aesthetic of California modernists like Neutra, Koenig, and the Eameses.

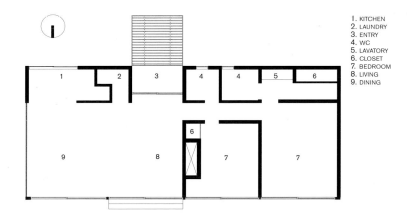

1. KITCHEN
2. LAUNDRY
3. ENTRY
4. WC
5. LAVATORY
6. CLOSET
7. BEDROOM
8. LIVING
9. DINING

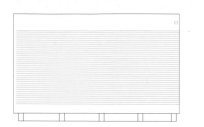
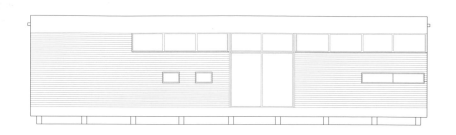

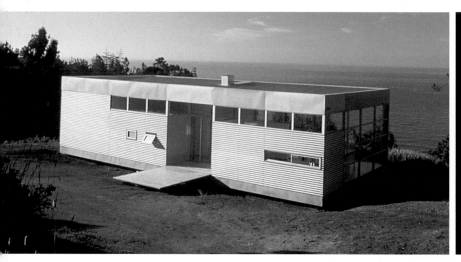

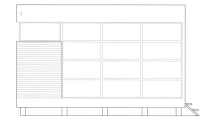

The house floats just slightly above the ground on a hill, and since the northern façade faces the beach, its sliding doors allow the entire house to open up to the exterior, making the ocean and trees part of the interior. The materials and finishes specified by Romero were chosen to accentuate the difference between inside and out. The zincalume exterior cladding not only provides this striking contrast but is a low-maintenance solution, too. Romero custom-designed stainless-steel furniture for the house as well as the kitchen, laundry area, and sinks.

Beautiful to look at, inexpensive to produce, the LV Home seems primed for mass production. As Romero explains, "My interest in prefab derives from my passion for efficiency in architecture. Efficient architecture must have a flexible program, be simple, and be cheap. It is keeping costs down that had led me to become interested in prefab."

Since the house's completion in 2000, Romero has continued her explorations into prefabrication with two residential projects that will utilize mass-produced components, and is researching ways to put the LV Home into production using prefabricated building technologies.

Vistet

Anders Landström and Thomas Sandell
Locations: throughout Sweden

Wood prefabrication systems have a long history in Sweden that dates back to the seventeenth century. The enduring appeal of this vernacular form prompted members of the regional Swedish government to consider developing the form for contemporary dwellers. The local councils of Jämtland and Härjedalen approached Anders Landström, a professor of architecture specializing in the art of timber, and Thomas Sandell, one of Sweden's leading young modern architects and furniture designers, to design a contemporary version of the traditional building type for a cost to the consumer of about $120,000. The concept was also intended as a way to develop log houses as a new local industry.

With a little help from traditional woodworkers, Landström and Sandell adapted the traditional Swedish log house into a more contemporary version that utilizes the traditional horizontal timber technique in a new way. The designers were interested in preserving the tradition of Swedish craftsmanship and design but not in replicating it, and their design lovingly incorporates historical precedents without descending into nostalgia. Sandell, who also designed a made-to-order prefabricated home for the design magazine *Wallpaper* in 1999, explains, "One of my own sources of inspiration has always been the simple buildings in rural Sweden, where people haven't had time or money to think too much about how to do things, but instead just went along and did what has come naturally."

Landström and Sandell's original design for the house known as Vistet Fritid ("Holiday Homestead") had a flat roof and an edgier look, but this early design was rejected as being too modern. The pair went back to the drawing board, reinstated the more conventional pitched roof, and eliminated some—though not all—of the house's contemporary details. "The log technique is unique," Sandell explains, "and should be used as a technique, not a 'style.'" The resulting Vistet was first presented at a home exhibition in Stockholm in 1998. Based on public response, a smaller prototype of the revised Vistet concept was developed. A prototype was built for H99, the biannual design and architecture show held in Malmö, Sweden, in 1999.

FAÇADE   END VIEW

The flat roof of the original Vistet was rejected for being "too modern." The revised version brought back a more conventional pitched roof and eliminated some of the prototype's more contemporary details. Its most traditional reference—the "haklak corner"—feels surprisingly contemporary.

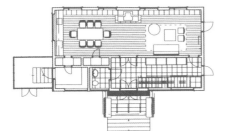

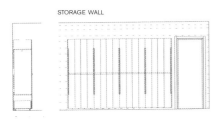

The final product is a kit house that can be erected and dismantled easily, allowing homeowners to take their house with them when they move. The designers took into account standard measurements of the Swedish logging industry in order to utilize affordable building materials. As in a traditional log cabin, logs were laid on top of one another and sealed with a V-shaped join filled with insulation. The logs used were 150 years old and obtained from local sources. (The house was produced in cooperation with the World Wildlife Fund of Sweden, and was the first Forest Stewardship Council–certified wooden house to be built in Europe.) The wooden nails that keep the strong logs together can be easily removed and reused if necessary.

One of the most striking details of this reinterpreted log cabin is the interlocking wedge-shaped joint developed by the architects. The "haklax" corner, thicker than others and self-draining, eliminates the protruding logs most associated with the form. The corners instead are flush, almost minimalist in their simplicity: this feature emphasizes the true nature of the wood. The architects combined the deep red color commonly associated with this housing type with light grey sides, a blend of colors designed to suit more contemporary tastes. "I always try to make the most from limited resources, which is the hallmark of most good Nordic architecture and design," Sandell explains. "In this country, we never had the means or the tradition for that matter to compete with Italy and other major design nations. We've had to settle for our simple materials and techniques, and we've been good at it."

Ideally suited to mass-production, Vistet successfully integrates a much-revered housing tradition into a contemporary dwelling that is flexible, ecological, and comfortable.

All photos on these two pages show the Vistet prototype house. Landström and Sandell's design pays homage to historical precedents without resorting to nostalgia.

Regenboogburt
("Rainbow Neighborhood")
Wickham van Eyck Architects
Location: Almere, The Netherlands

Regenboogburt ("Rainbow Neighborhood") is a new residential development comprised of forty-eight houses in Almere, a newly created town near Amsterdam in the Netherlands. The uniquely curving and colorful houses were designed to achieve a high degree of standardization in construction through the use of prefabricated elements of structure and building. Prefabrication facilitated more reliable prediction and coordination of building components in both the design and construction stages. The use of these techniques cut the cost of construction by over 25 percent as compared to traditional building techniques (the firm actually tested this through detailed cost exercises), and the controlled conditions of factory production ensured a high-quality building.

Quite simply, industrialized building "is cheaper, faster, and more reliable than traditional building when making large volume/scale projects," explains architect Julyan Wickham. But industrialization doesn't preclude individualization. Despite the standardized processes used, there is, within the basic framework of each housing unit, a high degree of flexibility in use and the potential for extensions/additions if necessary. "Each individual house is subordinate to the whole composed row of houses such that the row can form the street in one homogeneous move," Wickham explains. "Yet by curving the rows of houses, each house has its special and unique position and place within the street as a whole.

"The aesthetic can be and is independent of the method of construction if one chooses it to be," Wickham continues. "Our projects do not show in the least their industrialized and highly rationalized bones."

At first glance, they may all look alike, but Wickham van Eyck's innovative apartments look like nothing else—and allow for a high degree of customization.

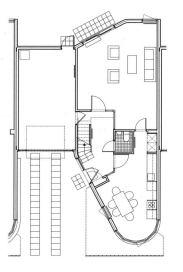

GROUND FLOOR

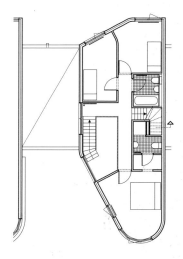

FIRST FLOOR

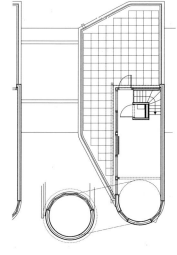

SECOND FLOOR

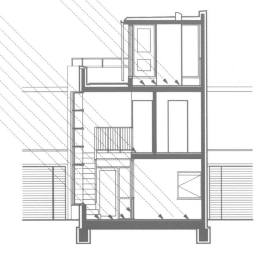

CONSTRUCTION PHOTOGRAPHS AND DRAWINGS COURTESY OF WICKHAM VAN EYCK ARCHITECTS

Each bright yellow house is planned around a double-height central hall that allows the house to be oriented in any direction. Despite the fairly narrow site allotted to each house (an average of nine meters), the architect found a solution whereby he could combine a strong street identity while maximizing the amount of sunlight brought into the house. The entry space lets in light even when the particular living room has a northern exposure. Each unit has a ground-floor arrangement of two living areas with the kitchen in between. The bedrooms, bathrooms, dressing rooms, etc., are positioned around the central hall, and the room with the tower on the top floor can be programmed as a home office, playroom, studio, or additional bedroom.

Wickham van Eyck's inventive use of component construction opened up many possibilities for the design of the houses at Almere. The same is true for several of the firm's other projects, which include a series of factory-constructed floating houses on the Regents Canal in London, a small steel-frame and panel with precast-concrete construction office block in the London Docklands, a block of flats using a hybrid system in Grave, Holland, student housing in London that uses a volumetric system, and 350 timber-frame houses in Dublin, Ireland. "Component construction will produce better and more adventurous design as long as the designer makes it his business to investigate and know about all available systems and techniques," says Wickham.

Prefabrication is cheaper, faster, and more reliable than traditional construction, especially in the case of multi-unit dwellings like this one.

PHOTOGRAPHS BY MARTIN CHARLES

Murray Grove Apartments
Cartwright Pickard Architects
Location: London, England

In Britain, as architecture critic Deyan Sudjic has written, "the very word 'prefab' is indelibly marked with the distant memory of wartime austerity, when returning servicemen were expected to start civilian life with their families in prefabricated houses erected on bomb sites."[1] Cartwright Pickard's Murray Grove Apartments go a long way toward changing that perception.

The Peabody Trust, one of Britain's oldest housing associations charged with housing those who cannot afford to pay market rents, was increasingly frustrated with the results of its conventional building projects. These structures were taking far too long to build and, once completed, were not of very high quality. Flying in the face of popular perceptions, the Trust decided to give prefabrication a try. Dickon Robinson, the Peabody Trust's director of development and technical services, explained as the project began: "What we are planning here is entirely different from the system building of the 1960s. System building was a crude matter of casting heavy concrete panels on a muddy site. In contrast, we are using a genuinely industrialized method, where the flats are almost entirely pre-assembled and fitted out in a factory."

Cartwright Pickard Architects was tapped to develop a prototype in prefabricated housing using modular or volumetric construction. If it worked, thought the Peabody Trust, a new system of housing would be let loose against the country's dire housing shortage. Partner James Pickard, who spent many years researching prefabrication and had many opinions about Britain's housing practices, was eager to jump in. The benefits of prefab are many, he explains, running down a list that includes "speed, half-time spent on-site, a factory-quality product, predictability, the ability to test building performance before starting work on-site, minimum impact on adjacent properties, and a clean and safer construction method."

The thirty-unit building's single-bedroom flats are made up of two 8 x 3.2-meter modules; two-bedroom units are comprised of three modules. All seventy-four of the modules required for the five-story unit on

The sponsors of Murray Grove wanted to create affordable housing in one of the world's most expensive cities. The sophisticated design transforms the notion of "affordable housing" into something people are happy to live in. The building's success with tenants, other architects, and the building industry has resulted in numerous new commissions for similar prefabricated housing schemes for the Cartwright Pickard practice.

1. DEYAN SUDJIC. "THE MODULAR INVASION," DWELL, APRIL 2001, P. 38.

The light, steel-framed boxes developed by Cartwright Pickard were
designed with the same dimensions as standard hotel-room modules so
they could be manufactured on existing production lines. Once fabricated,
the modules were delivered to the site and then hoisted by crane for
assembly. The entire building was erected in less than two weeks.

Shepherdess Walk in east London were manufactured by Yorkon Limited, a British company specializing in the fabrication of budget hotels and fast-food restaurants. The light, steel-framed boxes developed by Cartwright Pickard were designed with the same dimensions as Yorkon's standard hotel-room modules so they could be manufactured on the company's existing production lines. The money saved by building quickly allowed the remaining funds to be put toward good-quality doors, windows, and fixtures as well as fittings that were screwed in place at the factory. Once fabricated, the modules for Murray Grove were delivered to the site and then hoisted by crane for assembly. The entire building was erected in just ten days and, in theory, can be taken apart as quickly and easily as it was put together.

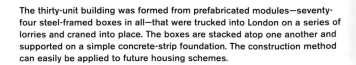

The thirty-unit building was formed from prefabricated modules—seventy-four steel-framed boxes in all—that were trucked into London on a series of lorries and craned into place. The boxes are stacked atop one another and supported on a simple concrete-strip foundation. The construction method can easily be applied to future housing schemes.

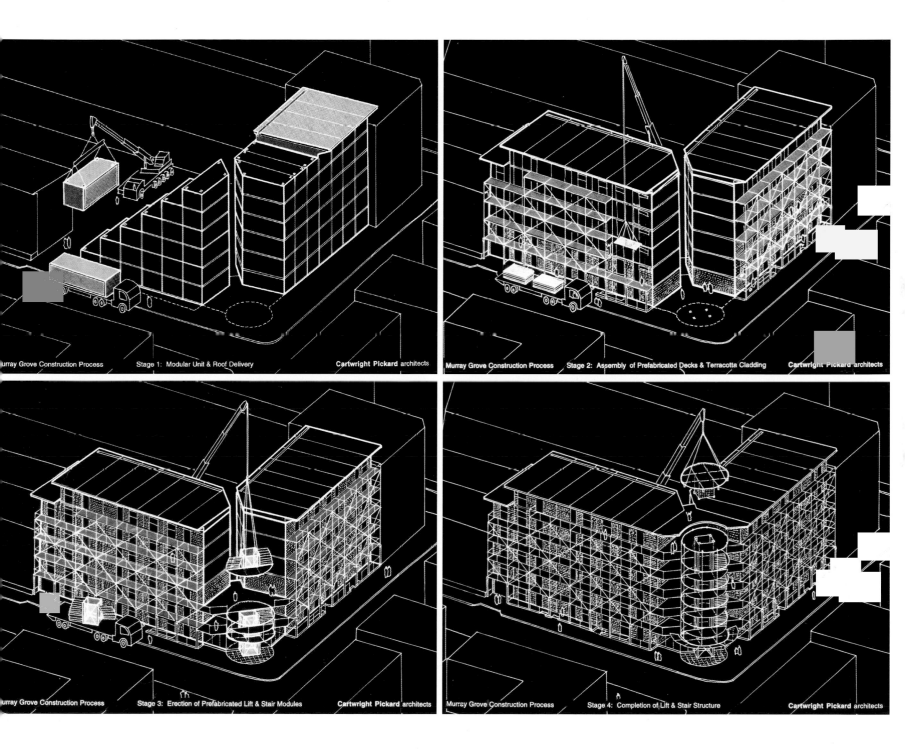

Murray Grove Construction Process   Stage 1: Modular Unit & Roof Delivery   **Cartwright Pickard** architects

Murray Grove Construction Process   Stage 2: Assembly of Prefabricated Decks & Terracotta Cladding   **Cartwright Pickard** architects

Murray Grove Construction Process   Stage 3: Erection of Prefabricated Lift & Stair Modules   **Cartwright Pickard** architects

Murray Grove Construction Process   Stage 4: Completion of Lift & Stair Structure   **Cartwright Pickard** architects

73

The building's exteriors are clad with a clip-on terra-cotta rain-screen cladding system and the roof is comprised of steel panels. Perforated aluminum screens form a translucent veil in front of the balconies and stair tower. The roof, distinctive circular entrance, and stairwell were delivered to the site as modular elements. The elevator and stair tower were also hoisted into position by crane. To save space, internal corridors were eliminated. Instead, tenants enter their apartments via street-facing external balconies. All flats include private balconies that look out onto a communal garden, and range in size from 600 to 800 square feet.

Murray Grove was incredibly well received, garnering awards nationwide, including the Royal Institute of British Architects' (RIBA) Building of the Year Award in 2000. "We now have approximately thirty million pounds worth of new modular-housing projects with Peabody alone," Pickard explains, "and many other new prefabricated jobs, including social housing for other clients, private housing, offices, student housing, and worker housing. Murray Grove has definitely created a large ripple in the U.K. market that is unstoppable."

By using prefabrication, the architects had money left over for details like the curved balconies that overlook the inner courtyard. A typical Murray Grove kitchen (top right). Bottom right, a schematic cutaway detailing the building's series of connections: modular wall components, pre-cast concrete access deck, and balcony handrail system.

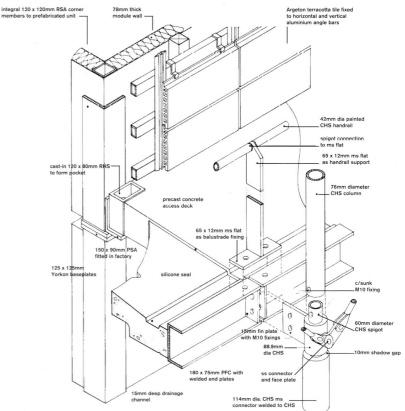

integral 120 x 120mm RSA corner members to prefabricated unit

78mm thick module wall

Argeton terracotta tile fixed to horizontal and vertical aluminium angle bars

42mm dia painted CHS handrail

spigot connection to ms flat

65 x 12mm ms flat as handrail support

cast-in 120 x 80mm RHS to form pocket

76mm diameter CHS column

precast concrete access deck

65 x 12mm ms flat as balustrade fixing

150 x 90mm PSA fitted in factory

125 x 125mm Yorkon baseplates

silicone seal

c/sunk M10 fixing

60mm diameter CHS spigot

15mm fin plate with M10 fixings

88.9mm dia CHS

10mm shadow gap

180 x 75mm PFC with welded end plates

ss connector and face plate

15mm deep drainage channel

114mm dia. CHS ms connector welded to CHS

Kennedy Residence

Anderson Anderson
Location: Fox Island, Washington

Brothers Mark and Peter Anderson of Anderson Anderson Architecture in Seattle are architects who are not afraid to get their hands dirty—and it shows in their craftsmanship. When asked what influences their work most, Peter answers that it's their time spent doing hands-on construction, talking to carpenters, and dealing with suppliers. The systems they've developed illustrate their deep knowledge of building.

"We're interested in prefabrication both in terms of mass production and site adaptability," explains architect Peter Anderson. "We don't necessarily expect that the market is there to make something 100,000 times the same way. We take the opportunity to do research by doing one-off applications to various systems approaches. Everything we work on, we're always thinking of it as a bigger system."

Case in point is the balloon-frame panel system that Anderson Anderson has utilized in both single-family homes and multi-family dwellings. "The balloon-frame panel technique is a basic premise of our work," Anderson explains. "By working on rationalizing the system of the production of the parts, we can then look for ways to adapt it. This system is extremely adaptable, even up to the last minute."

The architects have used the balloon-frame system for multi-family housing and for several custom homes in Washington and Japan, including the distinctive Kennedy residence on Fox Island, Washington. "We'd been working on things like this in Japan and wanted to try this panel approach but didn't want to do it in a remote location that wasn't under our control," Anderson explains. "The [Kennedy] site didn't lend itself to on-site fabrication so it was an opportunity for us to implement a custom application of the system. This house is prefabricated and a prototype, but it has the flexibility of being somewhat custom."

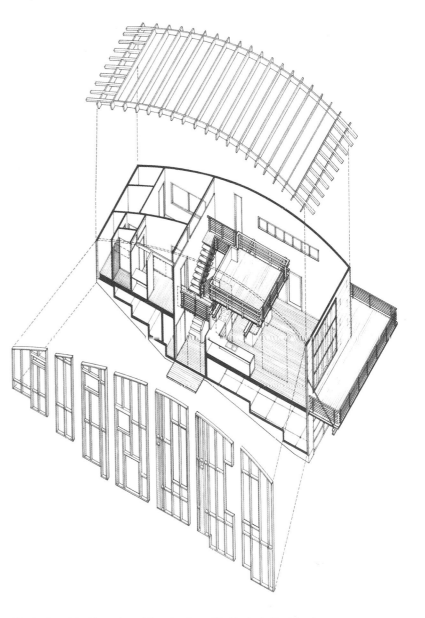

The incline of the Kennedy residence's site on Washington's Fox Island was the obstacle-turned-inspiration for Anderson Anderson's panelized building system. At left, a wall panel is lowered by crane onto the foundation and anchored. Above, exploded view of components.

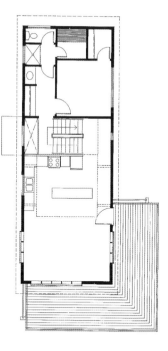

SECOND FLOOR

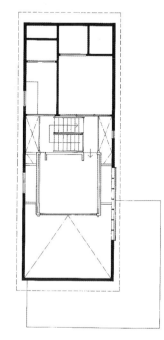

GROUND FLOOR

The panel system used on this 956-square-foot house was built five or ten miles away and then delivered to the site. The width and length of the delivery truck determined their dimensions. Once the prefabricated panels arrived, it took only eight hours to install them. (The light- and dark-gray-asphalt checkerboard tile took a little longer.)

Though the firm has become increasingly associated with the various systems of components they've developed in the last decade, prefabrication is not an automatic choice for projects, explains Anderson. "You have to consider what the optimal set of conditions is for creating the end product and designing for the process rather than coming up with a design and figuring out how to get it built. We're always thinking of it as part of a bigger system. There is a great possibility for a larger mass-production of buildings and building components. I think that the expansion will happen with components rather than buildings. That's the appeal of mass customization. There's still adaptability, but you're taking advantage of the production efficiencies of larger-scale production. You can repeat the same system without having it end up being the exact same product."

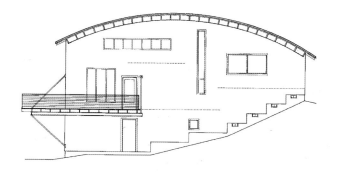

ELEVATION

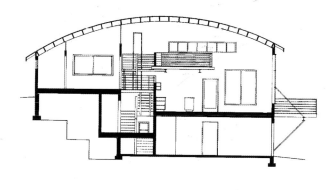

SECTION

The 956-square-foot panelized house was the architects' first home prototype. They were interested in creating a system that could adapt to individual site requirements and to the individual needs of the client.

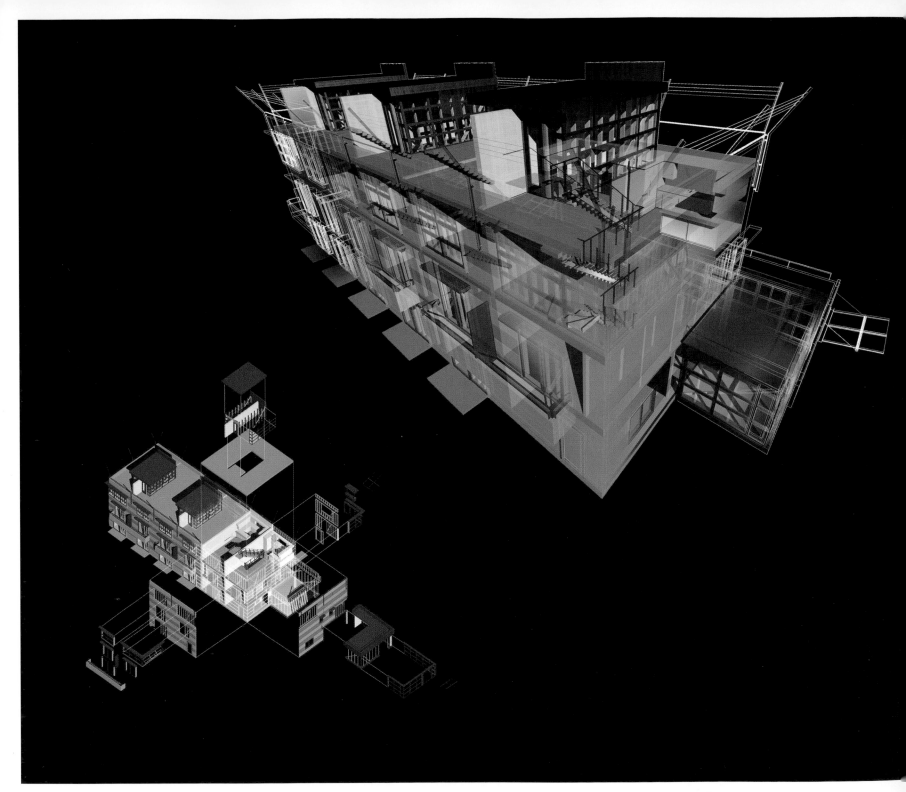

RENDERINGS BY MARK AND PETER ANDERSON

Affordable Apartment Prototype

Anderson Anderson
Location: Chiba, Japan (unbuilt)

The Chiba prototype was an important breakthrough project for Anderson Anderson, one which took advantage of a new loosening of Japanese building codes that had previously excluded three-story wood-frame buildings. "It was a prototype for the idea that you could have multiple units and that everything could be fabricated, brought to the site, and quickly put together," Peter Anderson explains. "And it took advantage of certain tax incentives that Japan was granting for affordable housing."

For the multi-unit apartment project, the architects created a variety of dwelling types and retail spaces on a small site sandwiched between train tracks, a temple cemetery, and an area with a dense concentration of traditional houses and rice farms. Flats for the elderly and disabled are located on the ground level with two-story townhouse apartments above. "The client wanted affordable housing but he also wanted to make a community," Anderson explains. In response to that, the architects designed a loft-like living environment with flow-through ventilation, an abundance of natural light, and lots of outdoor space provided by terraces, balconies, and roof decks.

The concept utilizes the same vertical panel system used for the Kennedy house where the studs run through the openings to give a flexibility to the windows and doors. The system's versatility is made all the more evident when one looks at the variety of structures the Andersons have applied it to. "You can repeat the same system without having it end up being the exact same product." says Peter. "To me that's the difference between last century's approach and the potential future use of prefabrication."

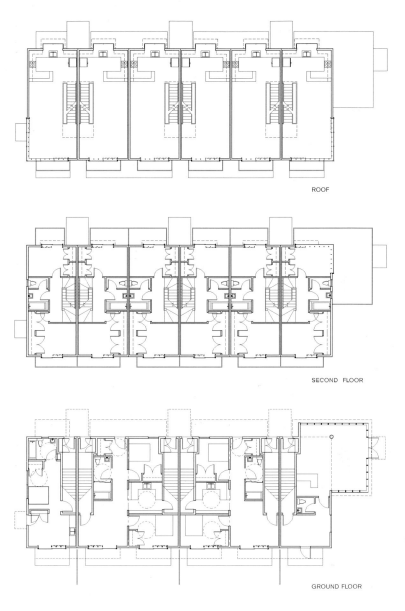

ROOF

SECOND FLOOR

GROUND FLOOR

In this concept for a multi-family dwelling, the ground floor would be home to elderly and disabled residents. Anderson Anderson used off-site fabrication in their exploration into more progressive ideas about elderly and disabled housing.

CUSTOM

Unique homes by architects less interested in the mass production of houses than in the aesthetic, environmental, and economic benefits of prefabrication.

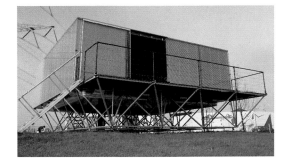

PHOTOGRAPH BY REINHARD ZIMMERMAN

Trüb House
Angelil Graham Pfenninger Scholl
Location: Horgen, Zurich

Completed in 1998, the Trüb House is comprised of two houses, one atop the other. The ground-level house is made of wood; its subterranean counterpart is made of concrete. The roof of the wooden house is made from insulated wooden plates supported by walls constructed of thirty prefabricated panels. These panels were developed into a sandwich construction composed of larch slats, painted plywood, recycled-paper insulation, wood studs, and gypsum board. Fifteen percent of the larch slats are mounted on sliding tracks, allowing them to function as movable sunshades and as a security gate for the house's vertical windows.

While the primary living spaces are in the upper building, there is an additional living space along with a garage in the concrete house. The lower building also utilized prefabricated building systems: it was constructed from seven prefabricated concrete beams sitting atop walls made from poured concrete. To maintain the volumetric singularity of each construction, a shear shift in plan was used to create a gap that runs the length of the building. This provides the effect of one house floating above the other and also helps provide sufficient natural lighting for the lower structure.

PHOTOGRAPH BY GASTON WICKY

"Prefabrication is one of many potential techniques to be deployed," explains architect Reto Pfenninger, who saw it as a way to optimize the design and construction of this sleek and modern home.

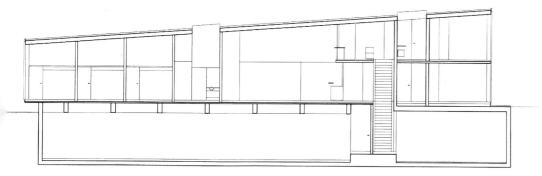

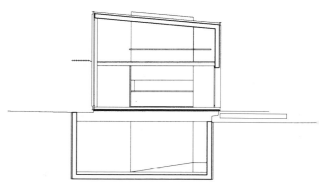

PHOTOGRAPH BY GASTON WICKY

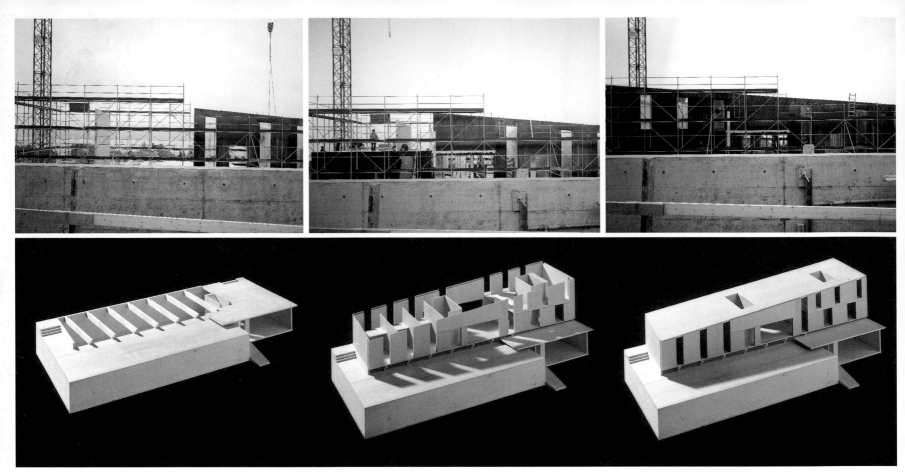

PHOTOGRAPHS BY REINHARD ZIMMERMAN

GROUND FLOOR

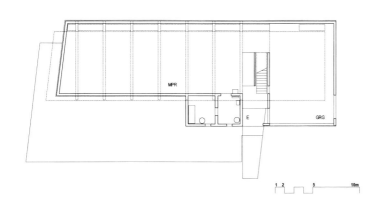

MPR

E   GRG

1 2   5   10m

FIRST FLOOR

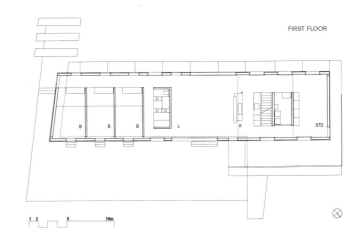

B   B   B   L   K   STD

1 2   5   10m

Why prefab for a custom home? "The techniques and processes used in construction have a determining effect on the created product in architecture as well as in other disciplines," architect Reto Pfenninger says. "Prefabrication is one of many potential techniques to be deployed. It was historically used to optimize fabrication procedures, such as in the work of Konrad Wachsmann and Jean Prouvé." With their building, Pfenninger and his colleagues at Angelil Graham Pfenninger Scholl have built on the techniques of traditional fabrication and the influences of modernists like Prouvé, combining them with digital technology to explore new possibilities. "Computer-aided manufacturing, first developed in other fields, has increasingly been adopted by the building industry," Pfenninger explains. "Such development has not only contributed to a further advancement of prefabrication processes in architecture, but has also promoted new spatial and formal expressions." With its solid construction and elegant form, the Trüb House demonstrates the extent to which conventional prefabrication techniques can be applied to architect-designed homes.

The house is comprised of two volumes, one wood, one concrete. Above, the concrete "house" underneath the main house contains additional living space and the garage.

MEZZANINE

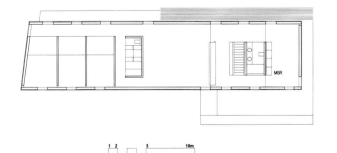

1 2   5   10m

Benthem House

Benthem Crouwel Architects
Location: Amsterdam, The Netherlands

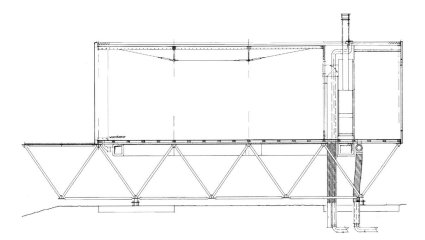

The architecture competition was wide open. Participants were not given a specific brief nor were they required to comply with building codes and regulations (with the exception of structural and fire precautions). The prize? A free site on which to build. The condition? The house had to be dismantled and removed after five years.

Rather than build an inexpensive house that could be easily demolished at the end of the designated time, Dutch architects Jan Benthem and Mels Crouwel decided at the eleventh hour to design a house that could be moved somewhere else when its time was up. "For me," Jan Benthem explains, "designing and building the house was not so much an experiment in designing a new type of housing that could be prefabricated in large numbers as it was an exercise in using an absolute minimum in terms of program, materials, and weight. There was a simple reason for that—the house had a limited period to spend on the site so it had to be very cheap or relocatable. And it had to be strong and light."

Concrete piling—the normal means of foundation in the Netherlands—was not allowed on the proposed site, so Benthem created a proprietary steel space frame to support the house instead. The frame consisted of octagonal connectors made from 5-mm welded-steel plate. The space frame, sitting on four precast-concrete industrial-flooring slabs placed directly on the ground, was bolted to the slab. The floor decking consisted of composite panels made from high-density polyurethane foam faced on both sides with plywood, which is normally used for refrigeration-truck bodies. Solid walls and partitions were constructed from the same composite panels. The walls of the main living space consisted entirely of 12-mm-thick panels of reinforced glass and acted as the main support for the roof deck. The glass panels were bedded in steel U-sections with clear silicone sealant in glass-to-glass joints. The roof deck was constructed from a .75-mm corrugated-steel sheet.

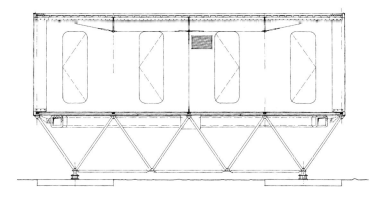

The house, seen from the back in its original location. Originally designed for a competition, the container of glass and steel was later transported to a new location where it was reborn as the architect's family home.

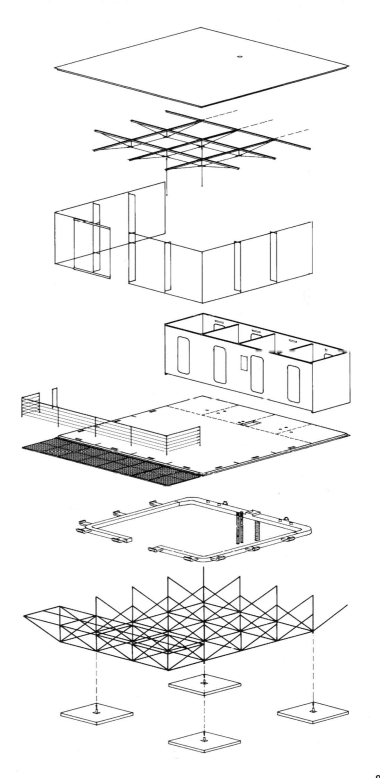

At the end of its five-year run, the house took on a new life—it became the permanent home of Benthem and his family. (They moved it to a new site and added a container for extra storage space.)

"This house was prefabricated because that was the best means of getting the lightest and strongest materials, and to be able to build it myself in a very short time," Benthem explains. Benthem Crouwel doesn't have specific plans in the works for other prefabricated houses, but uses relevant technologies as appropriate. "We continuously look for good, though not always obvious, solutions to design problems," Benthem explains. "We do not hesitate to apply modern technology in a user friendly way."

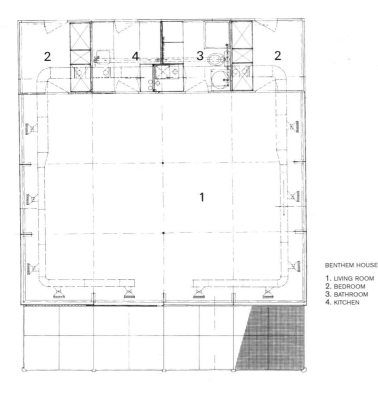

BENTHEM HOUSE

1. LIVING ROOM
2. BEDROOM
3. BATHROOM
4. KITCHEN

FRED

KFN Systems
Location: variable

"I always had the idea to sell prefab houses that would be cheap to buy, but would also have a certain attitude," explains Austrian architect Oskar Leo Kaufmann. Oskar and his cousin Johannes Kaufmann brought that idea to fruition with FRED, a modular home-building system that can be likened to children's building blocks. Though the components of the mobile container system come in different sizes, they result in houses that differ in square footage, form, floor plan, and detail. FRED can be expanded or contracted on-site: The exterior takes shape as the 5 x 5-meter modules are lined up or stacked on top of each other. Ten types of wall façades are available. The clients determine the layout and dimensions of each room in concert with the architects. The plan and design of each unit is then drawn up by the firm. Highly efficient organization enables KFN to offer short construction times for FRED (once on-site it can be fully assembled within two hours) and to quote a fixed price in advance of construction. Turnkey construction is available, though clients are also free to arrange for their own interior and finishing work.

Opposite and top, a version of FRED, featuring red veneer inside and out. Other options include blond wood with metal accents. The expandable structure houses a kitchen, bath, and sleeping area. The lower photo shows FRED with his "cousin," SU-SI.

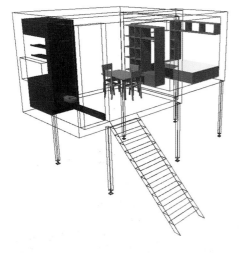

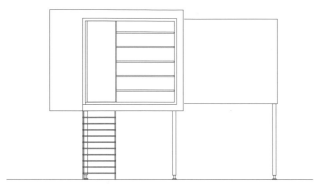

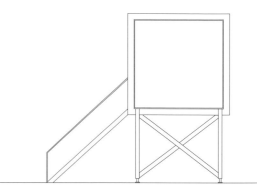

FRED, expanded to its full size, at right, is reminiscent of William Bushnell Stout's mobile metal house from the 1930s.

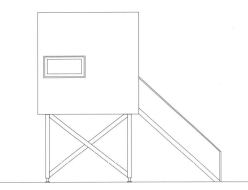

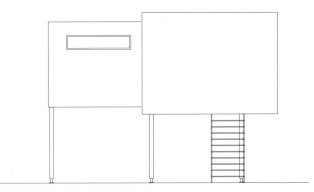

PHOTOGRAPHS BY IGNACIO MARTINEZ

SU-SI

KFN's mobile-home system, called SU-SI, was created in response to the firm's belief that conventional site-bound structures no longer fulfill contemporary needs and desires. Like many architects and designers before them, the Kaufmanns have been intrigued by the mobile-home vernacular. With SU-SI, they may have created that genre's best image makeover. SU-SI is a flexible structure that can be transported by truck, erected on-site, and installed within a period of five hours. It can even be placed on space-saving stilts to make room for a car underneath. Unlike FRED, it's not expandable but it comes in several different sizes, and both the exterior and interior materials can be customized to owner specifications. SU-SI costs around $50,000 U.S., and production can be completed in five weeks.

SU-SI comes in different sizes, ranging in length from 10 to 14 meters, and in width from 3 to 3-$\frac{1}{2}$ meters. Functionality aside, SU-SI's sophisticated design may have resulted in the mobile home's best image makeover to date.

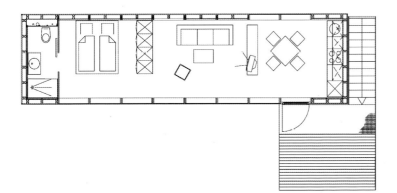

PHOTOGRAPHS BY IGNACIO MARTINEZ

Two-Family House

KFN Systems
Location: Andelsbuch, Vorarlberg, Austria

KFN Systems isn't limited to mobile structures like FRED and SU-SI. Oskar and Johannes Kaufmann are very interested in applying innovative methods of prefabrication to more conventional housing solutions as well. KFN's pilot project was this prefabricated two-family house in Austria that was built over a period of just four months. All of the components of the timber-frame house as well as the kitchen and bath units were prefabricated and then installed on-site for a total cost of approximately $400,000 for the two dwellings.

Since this home's completion in 1997, KFN has continued to build energy-efficient, prefabricated homes in Austria, and has begun to branch out further. In 2002, Oskar Leo Kaufmann and fellow Austrian architect Johannes Norlander launched two prototypes for affordable, wood-frame houses that can be customized to the owner's specifications and delivered by truck as a ready-made unit. "We don't see this as a design experiment," explains Norlander. "It is more an ambitious attempt to develop a small, functional, and affordable house for everyone."

Architect and client work together to determine the square footage of the house and the size and configuration of the living areas within it. The KFN system is designed to provide "turnkey" service but the client can, if he or she chooses, do a specified amount of the work on their own to keep building costs down.

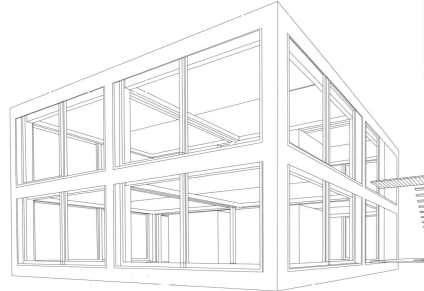

The building system, developed by the Kaufmanns with a group of traditional carpenters, utilizes modular timber-frame construction. Modules measuring 5 x 5 x 2.7 meters can be combined as needed to create a house of up to four floors. The frame, made from bonded, laminated pine, is fabricated first from 160 x 160 mm wooden beams. The exterior is constructed from ten different factory-produced walls, which, along with the ceiling and floor panels, are installed after the frame is complete. The panels can be chosen by the customer (much like buying a car with different available options).

KFN's construction concept proceeds from the idea of standardized building blocks, which can be reconfigured into houses of different forms, dimensions, and styles.

PHOTOGRAPHS BY IAN MACAULAY

Penthouse at Albert Court

First Penthouse
Location: London, England

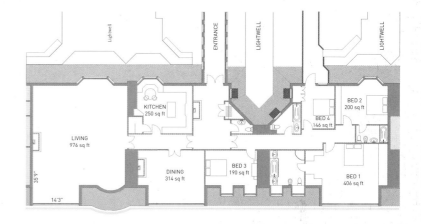

"Prefab" and "penthouse" are two words rarely put together. But with their company, First Penthouse, Swedish civil engineers Annika and Hakan Olsson have brought these seemingly disparate elements together in blissful coexistence.

"The rooftops of the central London skyline are a resource that has been left uncultivated for too long," reads the company brochure, "but one that is really only accessible if the heavy construction process is moved off-site." With property values soaring and urban density increasing, this is an idea whose time has come. As Hakan Olsson explains, "We got the idea when we were planning our own loft conversion in Stockholm. After having completed a traditional build conversion, it was clear that a lot of noise, dust, and general disturbance could have been avoided if the whole thing had been built off-site instead."

First Penthouse was founded in 1992. Since then, the company has developed projects in some of London's wealthiest neighborhoods, and plans for New York and Paris developments are in the works. The husband-and-wife team begins by negotiating a deal with a property owner to purchase a roof as if it were an empty lot. They then design the structure per customer specifications. The luxury units are assembled as modules at a factory in Sweden—a process that takes about ten weeks. After the units are outfitted and factory-tested, they are brought over from Sweden in shipping containers and lifted by crane to their rooftop destination. Once a module is positioned on the roof (which has been prepared for its arrival), it has a complete roof surface plus electricity, heating, and plumbing in about a day. The finishing touches on upscale, owner-specified amenities like fireplaces, hardwood floors, and custom kitchens take about four more weeks to complete.

The company is committed to a certain standard of quality but not necessarily to one particular look. "To me the fact that something is prefabricated will not automatically give it a specific architectural style," Annika Olsson explains. "The way we use our modules, and have to use them in

Modules arrive on-site fully equipped with heating, plumbing, and electrical services ready to be connected within a day. The units are also outfitted with customer-specified amenities, including hardwood or marble floors, wood-burning fireplaces, and custom kitchens.

First Penthouse's greatest challenge was changing the prevaling perception of prefabricated houses as cheap and unattractive. The spectacular views that come with penthouse locations like this one at Albert Court in London, combined with superior craftsmanship and high-end finishes, helped to dispel the doubts of potential buyers. Every unit was sold.

order to obtain planning permission, is to blend in with whatever style the original building has. The big challenge is to make it look like there has always been a penthouse. Therefore my interest is in any style and look that is appropriate for the site."

The Olssons believe that their efforts are having an effect on how the public perceives prefabrication. "Some people expect modules to look like Portacabins and be fitted to the same standard," Annika Olsson explains. With its superior craftsmanship and attention to detail, First Penthouse's version of prefabrication helps to dispel that notion.

These residences do have price tags commensurate with their penthouse status, factory-construction methods notwithstanding. The Albert Court units in central London, for example, sell for four to five million dollars apiece. The Olssons remain committed to serving this demographic but have plans to expand the First Penthouse concept to more affordable housing as well. Eleven penthouses have been built to date; twenty more are planned over the course of the next two years.

The company planned to build 10,000 square feet by 2002, and aimed to double that the following year. "The plan is for a steady expansion in the United Kingdom to start with," says Hakan Olsson. "New York is also a natural market. We believe that we eventually will be able to lower our costs by 25 percent. This will, of course, increase our market. Geometrically simpler and bigger projects will also bring the costs down."

PHOTOGRAPHS BY ROSS HONEYSETT

Bombala Farmhouse
Collins + Turner Architects
Location: New South Wales, Australia

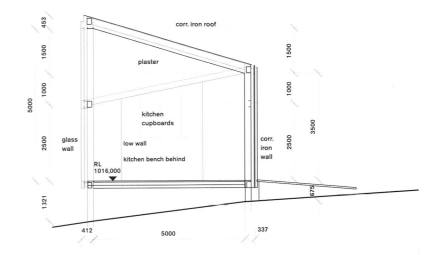

The combination of a remote location, a tight program, and the desire for a high-quality outcome led Collins + Turner Architects towards a prefabricated solution for many of the components of the Bombala Farmhouse. Designed as a retreat for a family on the remote Monaro plains of southern New South Wales in Australia, the house exploits beautiful bush, hillside, and water views. Set on a gently sloping long narrow clearing with views to both north and south, the corrugated iron, steel, aluminium, and glass structure is one house with two outlooks.

Penelope Collins and Huw Turner's decision to use prefabrication for most of the construction components was a logical one, as local skilled labor in the area (which is located approximately six hours' drive south from Sydney) was scarce, and could not be relied upon to achieve the high levels of precision and construction tolerances desired by the architects. Steelwork, glazing frames, kitchen and storage joinery, and furniture pieces were all prefabricated off-site to achieve the best quality outcome. When asked if prefabrication had hindered the creative process in any way, Turner emphatically replied, "Quite the reverse. The knowledge that we could fabricate precision parts of the building in a controlled factory environment and then transport them in a protected state to the remote site for rapid installation as part of the finished works allowed us to think more freely about the design."

The building is a simple, pared-down form, free from ornamentation. In keeping with the client's request that his house resemble a farm shed rather than a homestead, the house is reminiscent of the utilitarian farm structures that dot the Monaro landscape. The architects' design choices were also influenced by the local climate. Monaro's summers are quite mild, while winters are a bit harsher; so the very well insulated building is heated via an electric underfloor heating system. On sunny winter days, the exposed concrete floor slab acts as a thermal store of heat gained from solar radiation intercepted by the large glass walls, keeping the building warm through the colder nights.

"We were, and remain, fascinated by the ad-hoc agricultural structures that sit arbitrarily in the barren landscape of southern New South Wales." architect Huw Turner explains. That the architects are also fascinated by contemporary artists like Donald Judd is evident in the minimalism of the design.

The farmhouse's two primary spaces are unified by parallel blocks of equal length that run north-south: these blocks enhance cross-ventilation and natural light, as well as the views to water and hills outside. The slenderness and strength of a steel structure was required to support the large glazed walls simply and with minimal interference to the landscape. Says Turner, "Our goal for the Bombala Farmhouse was Donald Judd's idea of a specific object, a precision abstract form, set in a barren landscape. Decoration is omitted, everything is pared down, functional, and simple. In the end, only the abstract forms and landscape are to be remembered."

The Bombala Farmhouse was the first project completed under the aegis of Collins + Turner Architects. Much of the pair's knowledge of prefabrication had been gleaned from their experience working for Norman Foster's architectural office in London. "The Foster studio continually pushes the boundary of construction technology," explains Turner. A Hong Kong bank building the pair had worked on for Foster utilized entirely prefabricated service pods that were craned into position. Collins had also assisted in the development of a prefabricated cladding system of moveable aluminum panels while working for Grimshaw and Partners in London. And their collaborative partner, Ian Collins, who oversaw the Bombala project on the site, had designed his own house in Sydney in 1975 from prefabricated fiberglass panels, using processes borrowed from the boat-building industry.

Since its completion in 1999, the Bombala project has become the prototype for a range of projects being carried out by the architects. They have designed an "Eco-Resort" on the crest of Mount George in the Hunter Valley of New South Wales, and are also designing a range of kit houses for mass production for an American developer. Designed in a similar vein to the Bombala house, these prefabricated homes will be delivered flat-packed to site and should be available for purchase online by 2004.

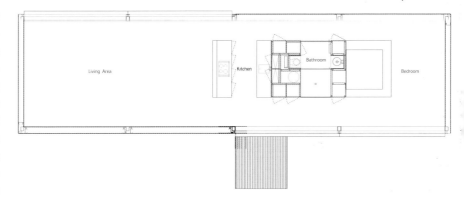

Materials were chosen for their longevity. Externally this meant using corrugated metal siding, structural steel, aluminium, and glass, which age gracefully and require little maintenance. The interiors consist mainly of concrete, stainless steel, and glass.

120

Furniture House

Shigeru Ban
Location: Yamanakako, Nagano Prefecture, Japan

Architect Shigeru Ban considers the properties of a given material and imagines how they can be reversed. He is interested in transforming common materials into something unexpected. Paper, for example, the most fragile of materials, becomes one of the strongest in Ban's work. In his Library of a Poet project, gate-shaped Vierendeel frames (the vierendeel-girder system is an assembly of floor spandrel beams and floor-height columns that are rigidly connected, acting as a girder spanning the supporting columns) were constructed from paper tubes and used to support the roof. In between the frames were freestanding bookshelves. It occurred to Ban that the shelves, which were designed to account for the load of the books and the stress to which the bookshelves would be subjected, could, like the paper-tube frames, support the weight of the roof. And so his idea for the Furniture House was born.

Furniture (bookshelves, in the case of the Furniture House) is an indispensable element of any dwelling. In this project, floor-to-ceiling shelves function not only as an element of space composition but also as the main structural element of the house. The Furniture House, built in 1995, uses two types of units: one is 240 cm high, 90 cm wide, and 45 cm deep. The other is 240 cm high, 90 cm wide, and 70 cm deep. These units, painted by furniture builders in a factory, were assembled at the site and joined to each other by a wood girder placed on their upper surfaces. Horizontal stiffness was secured by a plywood board mounted on the girder. This method is promising in its simple construction, preciseness, and lower costs.

Architecture is a continual process for Shigeru Ban, one that evolves from one project to the next. The first Furniture House led to another taller one in 1996, which then led to a third made of steel. Materials are used by the architect in unexpected ways—or not used at all. He is continuously interested in exploring the possibilities of a single open space with no divisions; indeed, his Wall-less House, designed in 1997, has no walls at all. Ban has completed four Furniture Houses in Japan and China and has developed a speculative and more expansive version (read: more square footage) for a planned development of vacation houses in Sagaponac, New York.

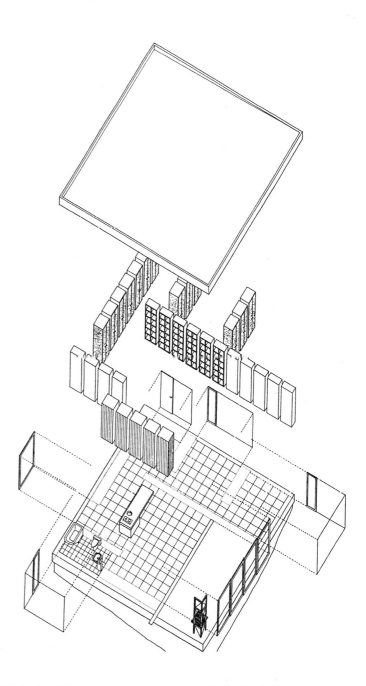

At left, the foundation goes up. Above, an axonometric drawing illustrates how the factory-produced units function both as structural supports and space-defining elements.

121

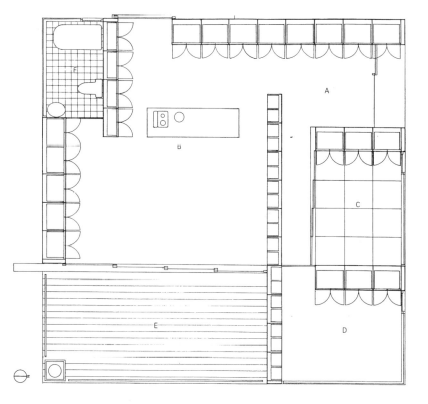

Opposite, the Furniture House's distinctive clear span roof. At left, top and bottom: Rather than relying on traditional beams, the structure of the Furniture House is supported by modular panels and floor-to-ceiling storage units. Above, the small cubes represent the house's prefabricated structural support units. Each unit weighs about 176 pounds.

Young Residence

Richard Wintersole, Architect
Location: Burleson, Texas

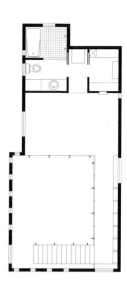
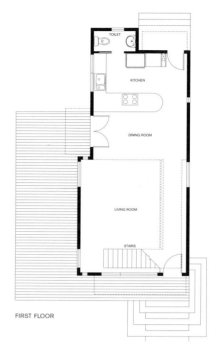

FIRST FLOOR

SECOND FLOOR

Building system manufacturers don't tend to employ architects, but that doesn't mean they won't fabricate something for one when given the opportunity. So when Texas architect Richard Wintersole approached Classic Steel Frame Homes, a manufacturer of building systems and components in Houston, with working drawings for a steel-frame house, they were happy to comply. "Most housing manufacturers don't really like to do custom designs because they can't crank them out as fast," Wintersole explains. "They cover up the frames and hide the fact that it's steel. But this company was just happy to sell me the steel." Classic Steel, a division of NCI Building Systems, fabricated a package that included everything from roof purlins to floor joists. The whole kit was put on a truck and delivered to the site near Fort Worth, where the parts were laid out in the yard like a set of overgrown Tinkertoys. Once the frame was complete, construction took approximately six months. The total cost for the 950-square-foot house was just $120,000.

Wintersole's client, Michael Young, became interested in steel-frame houses after he oversaw an addition to the glass-manufacturing warehouse where he works and thought, "Hey, I could do that with a house." Despite Young's strong interest in building a metal house, Wintersole wasn't sold on the idea until, when contractors' bids started to come in, it became apparent that a steel frame would be the most cost-effective solution. He went with a red iron frame that was bolted rather than welded together. The roof and floors of the house are supported by the frame; galvanized metal studs fill in the spaces between. And the benefits of prefabricated steel go far beyond cost- and-time-effectiveness. "The studs are straight," explains Wintersole, "and they won't rot when they get wet. No termites. And the frame is guaranteed to resist winds of up to 75 to 80 miles an hour, and in 'Tornado Alley' where the house is located, that's a plus."

Classic Steel Frame Homes fabricated a frame based on architect Wintersole's working drawings for this single-family home in Texas. This type of collaboration between an architect and the building industry is integral to the future of prefab.

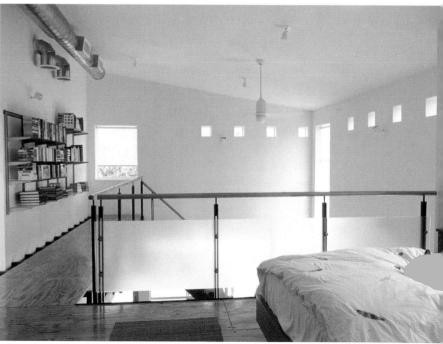

The frame of the house was fabricated from bolted red iron frames. The exterior is clad in white stucco and Galvalume siding.

Wintersole created an urban industrial loft space for his clients within the confines of a Fort Worth suburb. Interior details include sandblasted steel railings, diamond-plate steel stairs, and an exposed plywood floor upstairs, which the clients prefer to the more finished version on the ground floor.

The architect had a good deal of freedom in designing the house, as the Youngs' half-acre lot is located in an unincorporated part of Burleson, Texas, where standard building codes didn't apply. He came up with a clean and simple design for an industrial-loft-as-house that the clients loved. "I really love the aesthetic of steel," says Wintersole. "I can't understand why people want to cover it up. It's like telling a lie. You have this wonderful thing and then you cover it up. Being able to see the steel or any other building material, you're telling the story of how the house was built."

Wintersole has designed and built two more steel-frame houses since completing the Young residence in 2000. While he has no plans to develop a prototype house for mass production, this architect's successful collaboration with the manufactured-housing industry demonstrates the enormous potential that exists for customized prefabrication.

CONSTRUCTION PHOTOGRAPHS BY DAVID HERTZ / BUILT PHOTOGRAPHS BY CHRISTINA CLUGSTON

Tilt-Up Slab House

David Hertz, Syndesis
Location: Venice, California

"I've always felt that there wasn't a whole lot of challenge in just doing a building out of sticks," explains architect David Hertz. "It seemed an inefficient way to construct a building. There are so many stages. Once you have the frame up, then you virtually deconstruct it by drilling it to handle the plumbing and electrical. Then you go through a laborious and imperfect process of applying sheets of drywall, which again are individualized pieces with joints and seams that you're trying to disguise. And then going through all the scaffolding and ladder work. With a panelized or pre-manufactured system, you have far more control. There is much more interest in this project because of the tectonics involved, of learning this new building system, and of putting it together in these prefabricated pieces. That's where the thrill and challenge was, and I think that's what makes the house unique among other contemporary buildings."

David Hertz's innovative Tilt-Up Slab House in Venice, California, was designed in response to a set of difficult conditions. The lot was tiny—just 32 feet wide by 80 feet long—and on the corner of a narrow alley. The structure needed to house a couple, their two teenage children, and one grandparent. And the budget was $270,000.

"Given the confines of such a small lot, the volume was going to have to be a box, because that was simply the most efficient way to work within the building envelope. But because of the confluence of the narrow alleys and the lack of any views, I was really confronted with 'what am I going to do with this large blank wall?'" Hertz recalls. "If it's just stucco it ultimately doesn't have much interest. And wood in this area is impractical because there's a lot of moisture, dry rot, mold, a lot of termites." Concrete panels were the perfect solution. The house requires minimal maintenance because there's no painting involved and no layers to waterproof. And Hertz adds, "Cars routinely used to hit the house because of its location on this narrow alleyway, so its durability is a plus."

The tilt-up concrete methodology is the most economical way to enclose space on a large scale. That's why it is so ubiquitous for warehouses.

"Because of the confluence of the narrow alleys and the lack of any views, I was really confronted with 'what am I going to do with this large blank wall?'" Hertz recalls. Tilt-up concrete construction offered itself up as the most practical solution.

FIRST FLOOR PLAN

SECOND FLOOR PLAN

Hertz's design used fourteen six-inch-thick tilt-up white concrete panels that faced each other along the longitudinal edges of the site in order to create an elongated interior space. Eleven panels were poured off-site and then hauled in by truck; the remaining three were poured on-site and then placed in position by connecting them to the structural steel. The process took just ten hours. "It's not so much its form—it needed to be a big volume—but it's fascinating that the building arrives on a truck and is assembled," says Hertz. "That has a lot of appeal to me as something innovative and requires a certain amount of education in terms of reexamining the way buildings go together. The beauty of a panelized system is that you're actually designing the module. There's a more honest statement of what the material is throughout and that's especially evident when you're talking about a slab of concrete. You're very clear about what the material is. And it goes up much more quickly and can be more economical in a lot of ways."

To provide privacy and quiet for the inhabitants in a bustling neighborhood, windows were kept to a minimum. An internal ten-foot courtyard separates the garage building from the house. Natural light and ventilation enter the house through the almost entirely glazed front façade and

Hertz's design consisted of fourteen six-inch-thick tilt-up concrete panels facing each other along the longitudinal edges of the site, which composed an elongated interior space. The structure was erected in just ten hours.

through the double-height atrium at the house's center that culminates in an operable skylight. Radiant heating in the concrete floors, powered through the rooftop solar panels, allows the house to maintain ideal interior living conditions with a minimum requirement of outside energy. The result is a highly individualized house that utilizes the materials of commercial or industrial use. The costs are lowered, freeing up funds for finishing and details.

Hertz is not particularly interested in creating mass-produced housing. Instead, he is excited by the potential of prefabricated building techniques for custom projects. He disagrees with the prevailing perceptions of the low quality and poor design of prefabrication. The real limitation, he believes, "is that one has to appreciate the aesthetic. An engine block has a certain beauty to it and it was never conscious or by design; it was pure function. What I find quite beautiful is the honest statement of the parts. For those who are looking for integrity and an honest statement of construction and materials—well, these prefab wall systems can offer that."

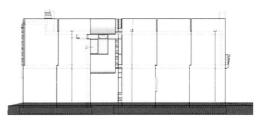

WEST ELEVATION

The house sits on a noisy and active corner lot, so windows were kept to a minimum. Natural light and ventilation come in almost entirely through the house's front façade and through a double-height atrium.

SOUTH ELEVATION

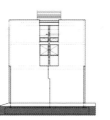

NORTH ELEVATION

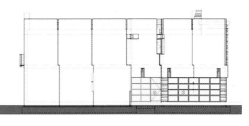

EAST ELEVATION

CONCEPT

A diverse array of virtual and conceptual prefab projects that employ everything from websites to neoprene in order to create the next generation of prefabricated housing.

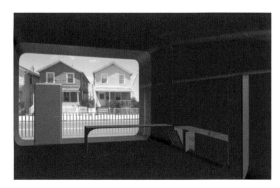

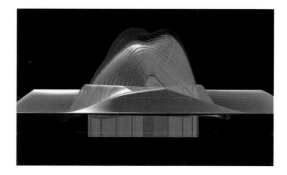

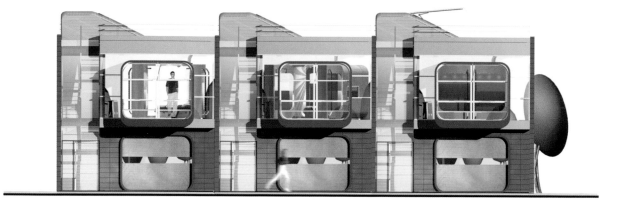

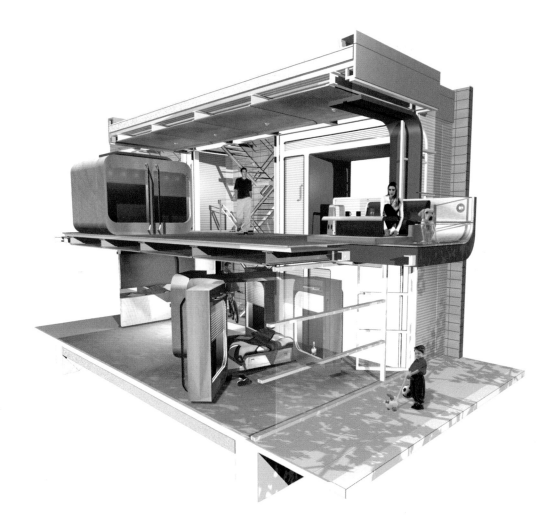

Shufl.e House / Microflats
Piercy Conner Architects
London, England

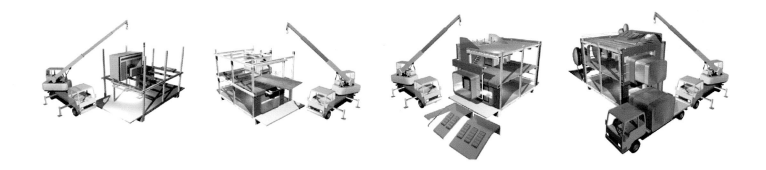

The Shufl.e (small housing unit for living) House, designed for the UK Concept House competition in 1999, is comprised of a series of fully integrated mobile pods that look, when installed, a bit like slices of a gleaming oil tanker arranged on the street. With Shufl.e, Conner envisioned a single-family dwelling arranged over two floors, providing a three-bedroom unit with a rear balcony, roof terrace, and lower-floor garden access. An open floor plan allows for different combinations of dwellings to suit individual needs and budgets.

Piercy Conner has continued its exploration of original housing solutions with Microflats. Despite the name, these compact apartments are not cramped but have been designed to allow as much open space as possible. Borrowing from boat design, the architects developed an inventive system of folding partitions, secret walls, and bathroom/kitchen equipment that allows for clutter-free living. Like Shufl.e, the Microflat aims to provide affordable housing for urban areas. Its efficient use of space means that more people can be housed within the same amount of space. In 2002, the Microflat was given a very public test-run when one was installed in the window of Selfridge's department store in London's Oxford Circus, and occupied by a guinea pig tenant for one week. The idea of an efficiently design compact dwelling seems to be resonating: A block of six Microflats are planned for a site near King's Cross in London, and the firm has submitted proposals for a block of 144 Microflats in Manchester, England.

The Shufl.e housing system is comprised of lightweight and wheel-mounted pods that can plug on to one another or be transported to another location. The "house" also comes with a detachable kitchen and bathroom.

RENDERINGS BY PIERCY CONNER ARCHITECTS

Flo House
Piercy Conner Architects
London, England

Architects Stuart Piercy and Richard Conner are passionate about prefabrication. For them, it provides the answer for smart and efficient building. Not only is it cost-effective, its aesthetic is well-suited to London, where the architects are based. To that end, Piercy Conner has created a number of creative and highly flexible housing solutions for one of the world's priciest housing markets.

Their Flo House, the first-place award-winner in the Velux Lifetime Housing Competition in 1999, responded to a brief for "a creative design which will inspire the next generation of mass produced housing." Rather than looking to historical precedents for mass housing, Flo looks forward by confronting issues at the forefront of contemporary concerns like sustainability, flexibility, and security. The resulting prototype incorporated not only prefabrication but sustainable technologies designed to reduce energy consumption and environmental damage.

The Flo House was conceived as a product to be assembled.

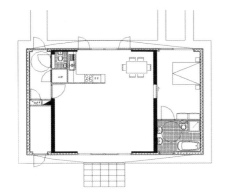
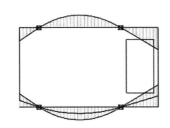
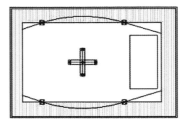

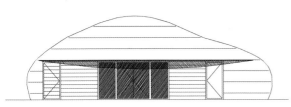
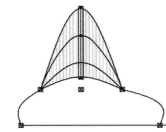

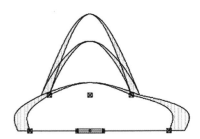

RENDERINGS BY KAS OOSTERHUIS

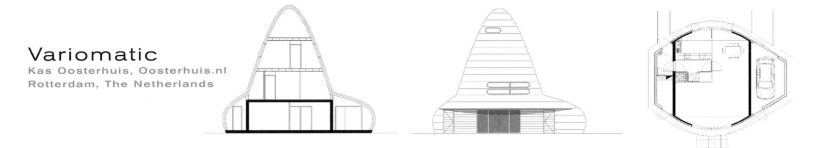

Variomatic
Kas Oosterhuis, Oosterhuis.nl
Rotterdam, The Netherlands

Architect Kas Oosterhuis has developed a prefab custom home for the Internet generation. All customization is ordered online. Oosterhuis originally developed the Variomatic project for a Dutch study at the end of the 1990s. The basic premise was to show that landscape, architecture, and consumer-friendly building can actually coexist. The results from that study are a response to (or against) mass-produced housing and the ready-made houses offered in master-builders' catalogs. Oosterhuis's web-based alternative to conventional catalog housing offers a way to reaffirm the identity of a region or a village, to strengthen a cultural landscape while providing the price, speed of construction, and freedom of choice consumers really want. After logging on to the firm's interactive website at www.variomatic.nl, the client chooses his/her preferred housing type. After shaping his/her own Variomatic house, the client can order a scale model or a set of drawings, or can even directly apply online for building permission if he or she already owns the land.

As Oosterhuis explains, "This new concept for a catalog house is elastic in all directions—in height, depth, and width—hence its name, Variomatic. The uniqueness of the project is that the clients are co-designers of their own house." When consumers opt for a Variomatic, not only do they define the final form of the curves (of the façade or the roof), but they can also determine the overall dimensions of the house, the location of the kitchen or bathroom, and whether they want to install a solar water heater." The client can choose from a variety of materials—reed, wood, metal, tiles, or PVC—and colors to finish the volumes. Through streamlined communication between buyer and architect, as well as architect and builder, and the advanced construction methods, it is possible to build the Variomatic very quickly while retaining the uniqueness of the house. As the home buyer is the co-designer, it is virtually impossible to create identical houses. "Variomatic offers actual styling instead of selling architectural clichés," says Oosterhuis.

Here's how it works: The standard plans of the Variomatic are organized in such a way that the warm middle house on the ground floor has two side buffers. These relatively cold zones comprise the garage on one side and the storage room and entrance hall on the other. The roof, with its overhanging cantilever, stretches as far as possible down to the upper side of the front and rear façades. The curved forms of the house offer the largest possible interior space with regard to the enveloping surface, providing its inhabitants with an enhanced spatial experience. The interior house on the ground floor is made of stone materials. Around it, a primary steel construction with secondary wood construction is finished with multiplex on the outside and plasterboard on the inside. The roof is clad with an ultra-light yet very strong and durable sprayed skin. With the groundfloor façades, the clients are given another opportunity to choose. For the surfaces between the wooden façades, all carried out in horizontal lines, they can opt for brick, western red cedar, or profiled steel. When the Variomatic is modeled and ordered, it is quickly prefabricated and installed.

Integral to Oosterhuis's plan is a respect for the landscape and an embrace of sustainable technologies. "Durable building starts with urban planning and landscape," he explains. The Variomatic is designed to make the best use of passive solar energy that can be obtained through the south-oriented glass panels and optional PV panels on the roof. The organization of the plan facilitates energy efficiency. Heat buffers on each wing of the ground-floor living area means that the house has less energy loss during the winter and does not get overheated in the summer. Respect for the land also calls for a compact and efficient space. Due to its rounded shape, the house can retain its own energy. The program also provides for flexibility of usage in the long run.

Though at present Variomatic exists more as an interactive web game than a tangible housing solution, Oosterhuis's ideas—client as co-designer, web-based rather than print medium, prefabrication applied to customization—may help expand the parameters of an industry that has heretofore been unwilling to take risks or directly address the consumer's individual needs and desires.

Siegal's new take on the trailer vernacular offers a much-needed boost to manufactured housing's less-than-stellar reputation.

The Portable House
Jennifer Siegal, Office of Mobile Design
Los Angeles, California

"What we're proposing is a rethinking of the trailer park and all the stereotypes that go along with it," explains architect Jennifer Siegal, principal of the Office of Mobile Design. "We want to reintroduce this new mass-produced housing type into that park and to create better environments by introducing light, opening up the interior spaces, and using more flexible and durable materials by making better use of what's already on the market."

In the early nineties, Siegal spent some time teaching in North Carolina, a center for manufactured housing. It was this experience that made her aware of the poor quality of design that was out there. "Seeing what was being constructed and realizing that we could do much better, and the materials could, in a very inexpensive way, be rethought, brought me to where I am today in my work. The technology and materials are available, but for some reason, they're not being utilized."

A few years later, a client approached her and asked her to develop a concept for what Siegal calls "the Portable House." Siegal, who had renovated a trailer for another client to use as a writing office, gravitated toward a refashioning of the trailer form. "I liked the idea of a contained, self-sufficient community," she explains, "which is what a trailer park is. The ability to live and work in a compact environment is very appealing and allows you to create a sense of neighborhood—something you don't get in sprawling communities."

The choice of a trailer as a jumping-off point was not surprising, given that throughout her career, Siegal has focused on various aspects of mobile architecture. Inspired by visionary housing schemes from Archigram to Arcosanti, Siegal sees endless possibilities in the Portable House. The 40 x 12-foot mobile structures she's devised are very compact but the same technology can be stacked for vertical expansion à la Paolo Soleri, of Arcosanti, who has suggested that we live lightly on the land, take up less space, and expand up rather than out. The structures can also be attached to one another.

The choice of materials is essential to the Portable House's eventual adoption by the building industry and popularity with the home buyer. To build these units at a higher grade, Siegal suggests making them more tangible, more acceptable. "If it's stapled together, if there's no fire rating, no one is going to want to live in it." The current prototype specifies Polygal (which provides excellent insulation because of the ribbed configuration of the sheets), structural wall panels (which use 80 percent less materials than conventional framing methods, resulting in lower energy bills), bamboo (a grass, which means that no natural hardwood trees are used), and Homasote interior siding made from recycled waste paper (its use decreases air pollution, uses 40 to 70 percent less water and up to 70 percent less energy than its alternative, and helps in the conservation of trees). Siegal's design concept also specifies a tankless water heater (which heats only the water passing through it), and a radiant electric heater, which uses up to 50 percent less wattage than conventional baseboard heaters. The adoption of other green technologies will be explored as the project continues to evolve.

To be sure, the living concept is not exactly a luxurious one, but it can, as Siegal explains, "exist in any situation. You're not bound or rooted to place. It's an idea that harks back to nomads through history. I see our society, and my generation in particular, responding quite well to that, due to new technologies, the global economy, etc. I think this project is a response to the way we live and work today."

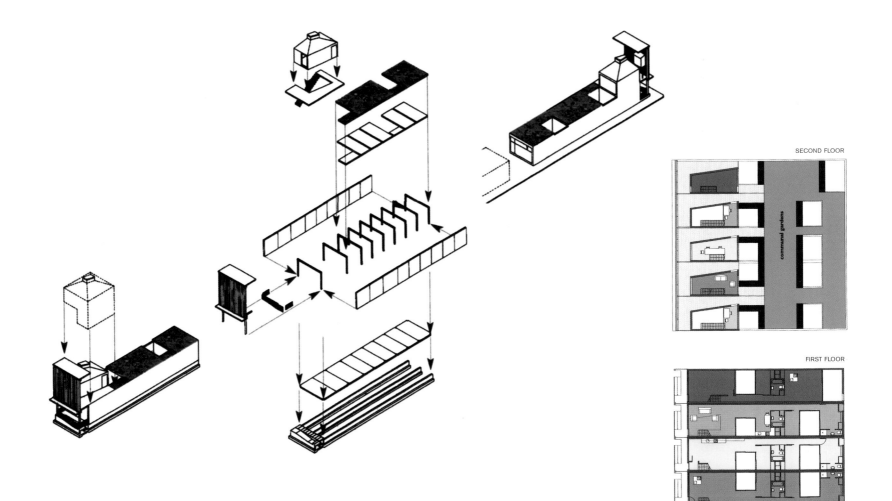

SECOND FLOOR

communal gardens

FIRST FLOOR

PLANS AND RENDERINGS BY PIERRE D'AVOINE ARCHITECTS

Slim House
Pierre d'Avoine Architects
London, England

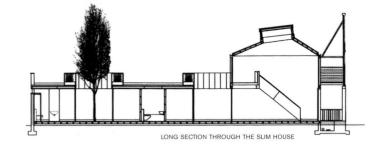

With the Slim House, Pierre d'Avoine and Claire Melhuish of Pierre d'Avoine Architects ingeniously reinterpreted the traditional British terraced house by laying it flat on its side. The design retains the scale of the traditional Victorian neighborhood while dispensing with nineteenth-century conventions that no longer respond to the needs of contemporary life. The customary three stories are transitioned into one elongated expanse and the lawn makes its way to the roof. Built as an exhibition house, the structure was a lightweight timber-frame: the plan for the actual house built on-site calls for steel-frame construction built on a concrete foundation. Each Slim House would be structurally self-contained, with the basic stability provided by steel frames that span across the width of the house. The floor and roof are made of preassembled panels of timber joists with timber boards on top. The roof of the first-floor study structure is constructed of steel bolted together and clad in similar timber panels so that it can be dismantled if necessary for a second-floor extension.

The Slim House was the winning entry in the Ideal Home Show's Concept House 1999 competition in Great Britain. The parts kit facilitates efficient mass production of off-site prefabrication at a cost of less than ƒ50,000 (approximately $80,000 U.S.). "The house of the future has always been set twenty to thirty years into the future," d'Avoine told the *London Daily Telegraph* after winning the competition. "But this house could be built today. In a way it's terribly traditional, but I'm not embarrassed about that."

Melhuish and d'Avoine cite as their influences everything from steel-frame agrarian vernacular to the Case Study Houses to Buckminster Fuller to squatter settlements in cities like Bombay, India. In the latter, the pair explains, "Discarded materials of all sorts as well as standard prefabricated materials are often combined with simplicity and invention to transform the most basic and squalid environments and conditions to provide their inhabitants with places which enable them to live with a certain dignity and grace." The modular design of houses and other buildings by British architects Richard Rogers and Norman Foster have also been a strong influence, but with their flexible, community-based housing,

d'Avoine Architects hopes to address in the Slim House what they feel are the inadequacies of those precedents, namely antiurbanism and lack of flexibility.

The house has all its main rooms on the ground floor, with two interior courtyards and a double-height living space at its front. The architects have conceived of the front façade as an active and engaging space—one with the potential to be developed as a billboard, a street light, a solar panel, a topiary wall, etc.—all subject to planning permissions and consultation with local residents' associations.

The plot of the Slim House is 5 meters wide by 25 meters long. The garden, in contrast to the conventional backyard spaces associated with terrace housing, is laid out across the roof and is intended for communal use. The roof garden nearly doubles the amenity space for each house and also encourages community interaction. Between the back of the building's three-story façade and the pavilion is an area designated for use as a more private yard. This rear space, like the front façade, is meant to be fully customizable based on the residents' needs. Each room has full-height glazed sliding doors that open onto paved, tree-planted courtyards, which bring natural light into the space and enhance the circulation and ventilation of the house. Each house has four rooms and two bathrooms, with an interior layout that can accommodate a variety of familial configurations and work arrangements. It is this inherent dimension of flexibility and change, suggest d'Avoine and Melhuish, that conventional models of prefabrication have overlooked in the attempt to reconstruct a model of a more permanent and solid architecture.

The firm is interested in an effortless, flexible, overall construction system that allows for easy recycling and redeployment of parts, which can be produced by non-specialist operatives.

PHOTOGRAPHS COURTESY OF OPEN OFFICE AND cOPENhagenOFFICE

NhEW (NorthouseEastWest)

Open Office, New York, New York, and
cOPENhagenOFFICE, Copenhagen, Denmark

In an age when everything from blue jeans to mattresses to fragrances is custom-made for the wearer/user, NhEW makes perfect sense. NhEW deals with architectural space tailored as if it were an item of clothing. It's a unit that adapts to the needs of the individual. A broad range of possible materials for different looks, climates, locales, and functions would be available to the consumer. The avant-garde shelter, developed by architects Tanja Jordan, Linda Taalman, and Alan Koch, is constructed of lightweight materials for easy transportation, assembly, and disassembly. These factors allow for endless variations on a theme and let the inhabitant customize the unit expressly for his or her needs.

The NhEW house project began as a research project in Thule, a region in the northernmost region of Greenland. There, nomadic Inuit culture has thrived for over a thousand years. The extreme landscape of Thule was a point of departure for the architects: they began to look at the conventional habits and mores of everyday habitation in order to assess the functionality and effectiveness of everyday life. NhEW is influenced by the nomadic culture of the region but is updated vis-à-vis contemporary obsessions like wireless technology and convertible clothing.

The potential dweller would begin by logging on to an online design site, www.nhew.net, where they would then specify their needs and desires for their own NhEW unit. The "house" would then be sent to the requested location in a single crate. The crate, measuring 83 cm x 143 cm x 203 cm, is small enough to be transportable. Once unpacked, the NhEW could be constructed within a day by snapping panels into place around the unpacked crate. The resulting one-bedroom dwelling measures 300 cm x 180 cm x 200 cm and can be used simultaneously, much like a studio apartment, as a bedroom, living room, kitchen, and storage area. Given its ease of assembly and transport, NhEW is an ideal vacation house, guesthouse, greenhouse, or house addition.

Open Office and cOPENhagenOFFICE enthusiastically embrace the materials of prefabrication—fiberglass, aluminum, resin-faced aluminum

At left, the transport and installation of NhEW in Thule, Greenland. Above, a view of the high-concept shelter—which incorporates elements as diverse as Tyvek and felt—ready for occupancy.

honeycomb panels, and Tyvek—but the structure is imbued with a heady dose of cosmopolitanism expressed through the use of more sensual materials like fur, fleece, wool, and felt. Each component is designed for multiple uses: clothing becomes storage, storage crates become beds, backpacks become furniture, packing materials are used as cushions and insulation. In recognition of the need for sustainable housing solutions, future NhEW prototypes will attempt to integrate functional energy, water, and waste systems as plug-in features. Photo voltaics, water collection and recycling, waterless toilet technology, and natural waste as fuel may also be featured in future NhEW incarnations.

NhEW is not quite ready for factory prefabrication, but its use of prefab-ready materials like aluminum and fiberglass, combined with the architects' awareness of the need for flexible, adaptable housing structures, broadens the discussion of prefabrication's potential.

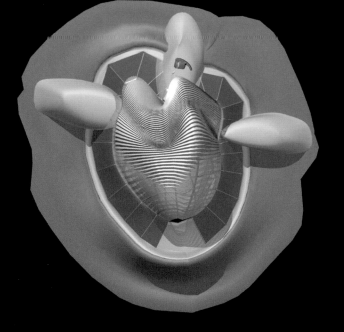

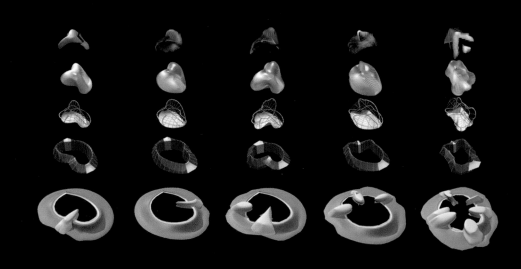

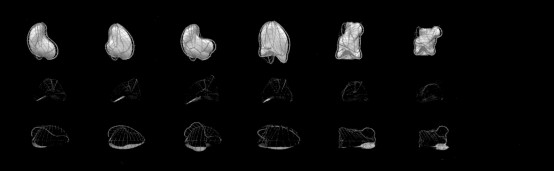

RENDERINGS COURTESY OF FORM

Embryologic House©™

Greg Lynn, FORM
Venice, California

Taking full advantage of new manufacturing technologies and sophisticated software, Greg Lynn's Embryologic House©™ concept offers endless possibilities for mass-customized housing. The variations available vis-à-vis computer-generated modeling are infinite, and even the site restrictions are few: an appropriate site is an area 100 feet in diameter on a less than 30-degree slope. Lynn projects a time frame of approximately fourteen months for design, production, shipping, and assembly for each two-story home.

As the project brief explains, the Embryologic House offers "a strategy for the invention of domestic space that engages contemporary issues of brand identity and variation, customization and continuity, flexible manufacturing and assembly, and most importantly, an unapologetic investment in the contemporary beauty and voluptuous aesthetics of undulating surfaces rendered vividly in iridescent and opalescent colors."

Lynn argues that modern architecture has conceived of the home as an assembly of parts or a kit. The contemporaneous technology of the modern period supported this notion: the industrialized assembly line lent itself to the production of a generic kit-of-parts house. The notion of housing as a minimum structure to which customizations, alterations, modifications, and alterations could be made fails to embrace the available media, technology, and creative processes currently at our disposal.

With its aluminum skin and monocoque shell, the Embryologic House has its origins in the trailer, ship, or airplane. But its relationship to such conventional structures ends there. The system of aluminum panels developed by Lynn and his team and generated via computer software allows for infinite variation in structure and form. Indeed, every element is inevitably mutated so that no two panels are ever the same in any single or multiple configuration. These mutating panels have been linked to fabrication techniques involving computer-controlled robotic processes in contrast to conventional industrial production. These processes include ball-hammered aluminum, high-pressure water-jet cutting, stereolithogra-

phy resin prototyping through computer-controlled lasers, and three-axis CNC milling of wood-composite board. These new technologies result in a "house" that lacks the right angles and rigid walls we associate with the term. Instead, the volume of the Embryologic House is defined as a soft flexible surface of curves—sort of the Bilbao of mass housing.

With the Embryologic House, as architecture critic Paul Goldberger has observed, Lynn has seriously attempted to "derive from digital technology a set of architectural forms as revolutionary as those crafted by the modernists."[1] Whether or not the structure will ever be thought of as normal or beautiful, as Goldberger wonders, remains to be seen. But Lynn's interest in applying the most advanced technology to the simplest concept—shelter—can only expand the conversation on what a house is. And what it should look like.

FORM team: Guy Bebie, Oliver Bertram, David Chow, Jefferson Ellinger, David Erdman, Andreas Fröch, Marcelyn Gow, Jackilin Hah, Matthias Kohler, Nicole Robertson, Hendrik Thiben, and Sven Neuman.

Opposite: A manifestation of "blob" architecture, the Embryologic House utilizes a system of computer-generated aluminum panels that allow for infinite variations in structure and form.

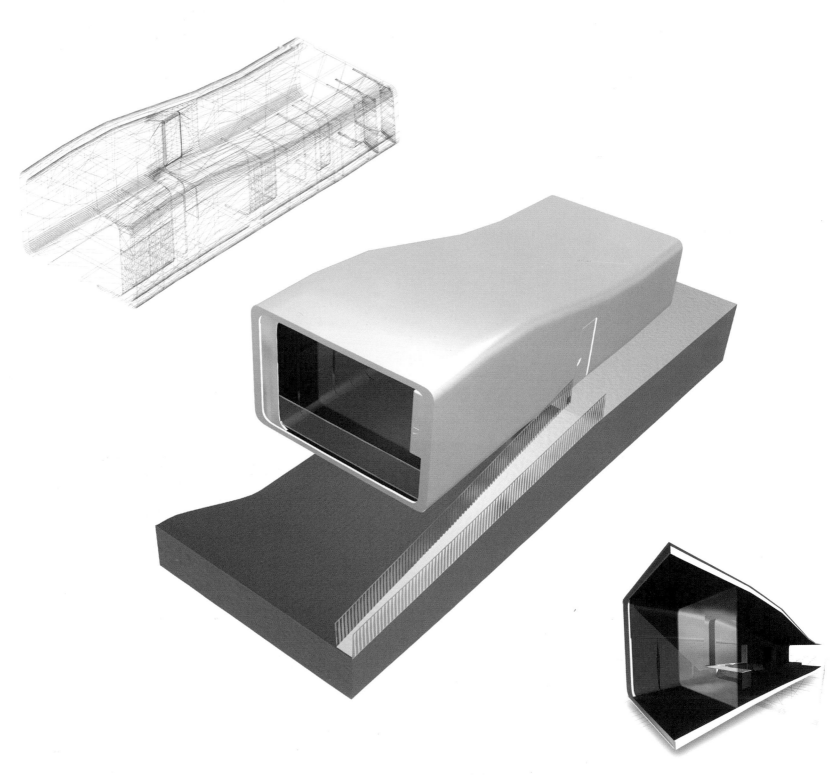

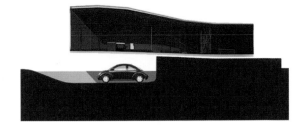

Hydra House
Konyk Architecture
Brooklyn, New York

"My initial interest in prefabrication arose from twin desires in the mid-nineties," explains architect Craig Konyk. "One, to begin to think of architecture as something akin to industrial design and, two, to try to 'standardize' the design process so that manufacturing conditions dictate as much what a design should 'look like' as theory or whimsy."

A competition that called for a concept to fill a twenty-foot-square plot of land in Atlantic City, New Jersey, gave Konyk a chance to put these ideas to work. Perhaps contemplating the legions of senior citizens who board the bus to Atlantic City each day in hopes of winning big at the boardwalk's casinos, Konyk's competition entry was a prototype for senior housing.

"The idea was to make a new model for independent living for those sixty-five or older," Konyk explains. "Like many of my generation, my parents are fanatically intent on avoiding the assisted-living route of geriatric communities and old-age homes. They are determined to think and act 'youthful.' So the idea of a swinging single pad really was what I was after, the empty nest as liberation, a loft-like space that allowed no nostalgic possessions, only built-in convenience, a land-locked Airstream fountain of youth."

But this is no old-age home. The Hydra House is a prototype for a single-room dwelling with neoprene-rubber walls—a material associated more with wet suits than senior housing. Designed to be prefabricated off-site, the house features a techno-savvy update on the Murphy bed: it has kitchen units and beds that fold up into the walls at the touch of the button. The notion of designing something that could be quickly assembled anywhere led Konyk to the exploration of prefabrication techniques. Thus the Hydra House features a sectional construction not unlike those employed by the aerospace industry. The result is an easy-to-maintain environment that liberates the retired person, freeing him or her from an overabundance of domestic concerns.

Red neoprene is not for the faint of heart, however, and Konyk's conceptual project, while generating interest from various parties, awaits a development proposal. Certain theoretical ideas have found their way into the real design of other Konyk Architecture projects, however, including the initial design for a beach house on Long Island, New York. The issues Konyk explores in the Hydra House expand our notions of what constitutes a factory-made home. As Konyk explains, "If this design has any effect on prefabrication, it is hopefully that prefab does not have to mean boring, standard, repetitive design, but rather can mean a fresh approach to seeking new solutions to those everyday issues of shelter."

Neoprene notwithstanding, Craig Konyk's exploration into the often-overlooked issue of senior housing is not only creative, it's refreshingly altruistic.

RENDERINGS BY HARMEN VAN DE WAL AND BART GOEDBLOED

Houseintheshed

Krill Architecture, Urban Planning and Research
Rotterdam, The Netherlands

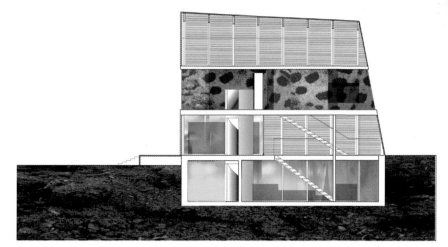

The Houseintheshed (Huisindeschuur) is a new housing type for private plots, developed by the Dutch firm of Krill Architecture, Urban Planning and Research. Krill's concept aims to combine the comfort and austerity of a modern house with the rough-hewn charm of a converted farmhouse. This is a concept house, and the precise materials and construction methods are not specified. However, what this house demonstrates is the ease with which standard units of housing can be customized and, by extension, made into more personal dwellings than conventional, mass-produced developments.

The prototype house, developed by architects Harmen van de Wal and Bart Goedbloed, consists of one simple volume: a box with slanted sides enveloping the house like a loose-fitting second skin. At the first-floor level, a central "chunk" is removed, and this cutaway section contains a living room with views. The house has been given a distinct appearance by its creators: their goal, however, is to allow the owner great latitude as far as customization. Both the functions and layout are adaptable and changeable. The house can be divided into two separate dwellings for parents with a child or an ideal live/work space for a single person or couple. The exterior is also replaceable. Like a Smart Car or mobile phone, the Houseintheshed has a highly flexible design that allows the occupant to select his or her desired style and finishing. While the structure is static, the exterior appearance can be changed simply by replacing the house's "skin." Krill suggests exterior options ranging from timber boarding to canvas sheeting to glass.

The project took first prize in a 2001 competition that was sponsored by the city of Rotterdam to inspire future residents of a luxury development in the new housing district of Nesselande. Those who opt for the Houseintheshed will, the architects suggest, "be able to give full rein to their territorial instincts here. People who live in it for an extended period of time will see the changes in their life reflected in the building." To facilitate this evolution, the structure is divided into a house containing the living room, master bedroom, and kitchen, as well as a shed that can be used for storage, a playroom, or a studio.

Krill is also developing a small, flexible garden house for mass production. It consists of three small cubicles, each 2.6 x 1.9 meters, that can be reconfigured at whim. "It will be possible to create a completely different dwelling every season of the year," Goedbloed explains, "from an airy and open house in summertime to a small compressed and warm house in the winter." The architects completed and installed the first prototype in van de Wal's garden in 2002.

Polka dots, paisleys, or animal prints? Krill's simple concept demonstrates the limitless potential for standard units of housing to be customized.

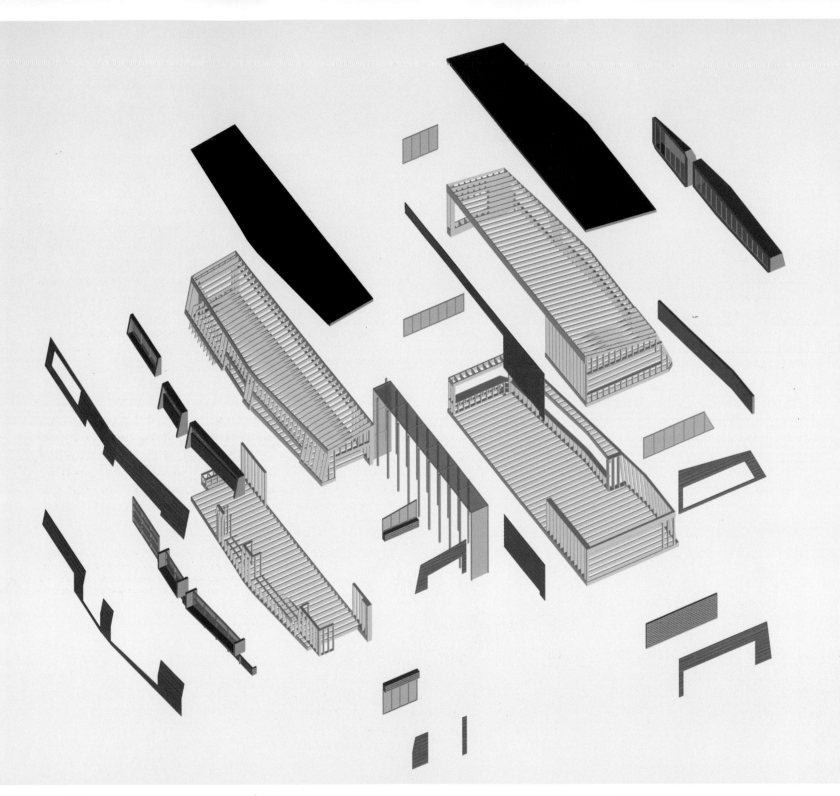

The Slide-Rule House

Choi-Campagna Design
New York, New York

The Slide-Rule House by Choi-Compagna Design is one of several designed for etekt (www.etekt.com), an online architecture studio that brings together the expertise of innovative, architecture and design firms from around the world, providing developers and private clients access to well-designed, affordable, and customizable architectural planning documents for new residential projects. Founded in 2000 by Bruce Fisher, Matthias Hollwich, and Mark Rosa, etekt describes itself as "potentially the world's biggest architecture studio." Etekt's inaugural design brief asked architects to submit house designs whose costs were comparable to the national averages for other similar-sized homes. It was essential that the houses be able to be constructed by the average builder/contractor with common residential components and materials.

Architects Sheila Choi and Adam Campagna took etekt's directive one step further with the Slide-Rule House by conceiving a design that could also serve as a premanufactured or kit-built prototype. The split design of the Slide-Rule House allows for each half to be premanufactured as an upper- and lower-floor module. When delivered to the site, the halves can be situated in different positions relative to each other.

The structure of the Slide-Rule House is basic and uses standard off-the-shelf light-wood framing components. This material choice allows the design to be site-constructed or premanufactured, dependent on client need. The firm is also at work on a steel-frame prototype meant solely for premanufacturing. In keeping with etekt's desire to offer houses suited to each client's preferences, the Slide-Rule House's exterior cladding may be any of a number of materials to suit the local climate or context. Each main volume has predetermined one- and two-story niches and bands that are carved out to define areas for potential fenestration. A variety of window and metal-siding configuration packages can be chosen to suit the house. As this is a concept house, the precise cost has yet to be determined, but the estimated construction time is eight weeks.

The Slide-Rule House can be viewed as a hybrid of the conventional two-story, pitched-roof suburban house. "By manipulating conventional residential typologies," the architects explain, "it is our intention that the house would create a more complex dialogue of form and materials with the others around it as opposed to a more stark contrast of a high-modern design. This strategy is also intended to appeal to the larger traditional buyer's market, while still providing room for formal innovation."

Opposite: An exploded view illustrating the Slide-Rule House's off-the-shelf components. The easily obtainable materials facilitate construction, whether in the factory or on-site.

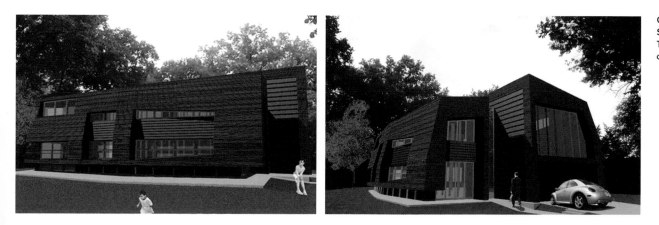

BIBLIOGRAPHY

Alexander, Christopher. *The Timeless Way of Building.* New York: Oxford University Press, 1979.

Anderson, Mark and Peter. *Anderson Anderson: Architecture and Construction.* New York: Princeton Architectural Press, 2001.

Arehart, David. "Mobile Homes for Defense." *Automobile and Trailer Travel Magazine:* (February 1942): 7–9, 12.

Baldwin, Jay. "We Dream of Prefabs . . ." *Dwell,* vol. 1, no. 4 (April 2001): 36–37.

Burkhart, Bryan, and David Hunt. *Airstream: The History of the Land Yacht.* San Francisco: Chronicle Books, 2000.

Carlson, Don O. *How and Why to Buy a Factory-Built Home.* Ventura, California: CMN Associates, 2001.

Cherner, Norman. *Fabricating Houses from Component Parts: How to Build a House for $6,000.* New York: Reinhold Publishing Corporation, 1957.

Conrads, Ulrich. *Programs and Manifestoes on 20th-Century Architecture.* Cambridge, Massachusetts: The MIT Press, 1970.

Cook, Peter, ed. *Archigram.* New York: Princeton Architectural Press, 1999.

Corn, Joseph J., and Brian Horrigan. *Yesterday's Tomorrows.* Baltimore and London: The Johns Hopkins University Press, 1996.

Davis, Sam. ed. *Forms of Housing.* New York: Van Nostrand Reinhold Co., 1977.

Dietz, Albert G. H., and Laurence S. Cutler, eds. *Industrialized Systems for Housing.* Cambridge, Massachusetts: The MIT Press, 1971.

Ditto, Jerry, and Lanning Stern. *Eichler Homes: Design for Living.* San Francisco: Chronicle Books, 1995.

Faulkner, Ray and Sarah. *Inside Today's Home.* New York: Holt, Rinehart and Winston, Inc., 1960.

Fetters, Thomas T. *The Lustron Home: The History of a Postwar Prefabricated Housing Experiment.* Jefferson, North Carolina: McFarland & Company, Inc., 2002.

Frampton, Kenneth. *Le Corbusier.* London: Thames & Hudson, 2001.

Gentsch, Fred V. "Decorating Your Mobile Home," *Trail-R-News Magazine.* (December 1954): 19.

Giedion, Siegfried. *Mechanization Takes Command.* Oxford, England: Oxford University Press, 1948.

Goldberger, Paul. "Digital Dreams," *The New Yorker* (12 March 2001).

Hines, Thomas. *Richard Neutra and the Search for Modern Architecture.* New York: Oxford University Press, 1982.

Hochman, Elaine S. *Bauhaus: Crucible of Modernism.* New York: Fromm International, 1997.

Hurley, Andrew. *Diners, Bowling Alleys and Trailer Parks: Chasing the American Dream in Postwar Consumer Culture.* New York: Basic Books, 2001.

Jackson, Lesley. *Contemporary: Architecture and Interiors of the 1950s.* London: Phaidon, 1994.

Jandl, H. Ward. *Yesterday's Houses of Tomorrow: Innovative American Homes, 1850–1950.* Washington, D.C. : The Preservation Press, National Trust for Historic Preservation, 1991.

Jodido, Philip. *Architecture Now!* Cologne, Germany: Taschen, 2001.

Kirkham, Pat. *Charles and Ray Eames, Designers of the Twentieth Century.* New York: Princeton Architectural Press, 1995.

Koshalek, Richard, and Elizabeth A. T. Smith. *At the End of the Century: One Hundred Years of Architecture.* New York: Harry Abrams Publishers and the Los Angeles County Museum, 1998.

Krause, Joachim, and Claude Lichtenstein, eds. *Your Private Sky: R. Buckminster Fuller.* Zurich, Switzerland: Lars Müller Publishers, 1999.

Kronenburg, Robert, ed. *Transportable Environments: Theory, Context, Design and Technology.* London and New York: E & FN Spon/Routledge, 1998.

Lambert, Phyllis, ed. *Mies in America.* Montreal: The Canadian Centre for Architecture and Whitney Museum of American Art, 2001.

Lamm, Michael. "The Instant Building," *Invention & Technology* (Winter 1998): 68–70.

Le Corbusier. *Towards a New Architecture.* New York: Dover, 1986 [first published in 1931].

Lynes, Russell. *The Tastemakers.* New York: Grosset & Dunlap, 1954.

Marcus, George H. *Le Corbusier: Inside the Machine for Living.* New York: The Monacelli Press, 2000.

–––. *Design in the Fifties: When Everyone Went Modern.* Munich and New York: Prestel-Verlag, 1998.

McCoy, Esther. *Case Study Houses: 1945–1962.* Santa Monica, California: Hennessey + Ingalls, 1962, 1977.

Migayrou, Frédéric, and Marie-Ange Brayer. *ArchiLab: Radical Experiments in Global Architecture.* New York: Thames & Hudson, 2001.

"Money Savers for the Home Builder." *Popular Mechanics* (August 1939): 194–99.

Monk, Tony. *The Art and Architecture of Paul Rudolph.* New York: Wiley-Academy, 1999.

Nulson, Robert H. *All About Parks for Mobile Homes and Trailers.* Beverly Hills, California: The Trail-R-Club of America, 1960.

Pebworth, R. C. "Trailers Grow Up Into Houses without Wheels," *Automobile and Trailer Travel Magazine,* vol. 3, no. 6 (1938): 13–15.

Pople, Nicholas. *Experimental Houses.* London: Watson Guptill, 2000.

Raab, Judith and Bernard. *Good Shelter: A Guide to Mobile, Modular, and Prefabricated Houses, Including Domes.* New York: Quadrangle/The New York Times Book Co., 1975.

Reisley, Roland, with John Timpane. *Usonia New York: Building a Community with Frank Lloyd Wright.* New York: Princeton Architectural Press, 2001.

"Reviewing the Tectonic: Architecture/Technology/Production" (ACSA East Central Regional Conference, Fall 2000, The University of Michigan, A. Alfred Taubman College of Architecture and Urban Planning, November 3–5, 2000).

Richardson, Phyllis. *XS: Big Ideas, Small Buildings.* New York: Universe, 2001.

Richardson, Vicky. *New Vernacular Architecture.* London: Watson Guptill, 2001.

Rosa, Joseph. *Albert Frey, Architect.* New York: Rizzoli, 1990.

Rowlands, Penelope. *Jean Prouvé.* San Francisco: Chronicle Books, 2001.

Sante, Luc. "It's Alive," *Metropolis* (April 1999).

Shelter. Bolinas, California: Shelter Publications, Ltd., 1973.

Smith, Elizabeth A. T., ed. *Blueprints for Modern Living: History and Legacy of the Case Study Houses.* Cambridge, Massachusetts, and London, England: The MIT Press, 1998.

Sudjic, Deyan. "The Modular Invasion." *Dwell,* vol. 1, no. 4 (April 2001): 54–63.

"Testimony Submitted to the Millennial Housing Commission," AIA Government Affairs, 2001 Legislative Priority Issues.

Wagner, Andrew. "Was It Motohome-o-Phobia?" *Dwell,* vol. 1, no. 4 (April 2001): 96.

Wallis, Allan D. *Wheel Estate: The Rise and Decline of Mobile Homes.* New York: Oxford University Press, 1991.

Zeiger, Mimi. "Some Assembly Required," *Dwell,* vol. 1, no. 4 (April 2001): 44–53.

ARCHITECTS + DESIGNERS

Anderson Anderson
911 Western Avenue, #511
Seattle, WA 98104
tel. 206.623.5108
www.andersonanderson.com

Angelil Graham Pfenninger Scholl
Zypressentrasse 71
CH 8004 Zurich, Switzerland
tel. +41 01 298 2020
architektur@agps.ch

Shigeru Ban, Architect
5-2-4 Matubara Ban Bldg 1Fl
Setagaya, Tokyo 156 Japan
tel. +81 3 3324 6760

Benthem Crouwel Architect
Generaal Vetterstraat 6
1059 BT Amsterdam NL
tel. +31 (0)20 642 0105
www.benthemcrouwel.nl

Bo Klok (IKEA)
Sodergatan 28
SE-211 34 Malmö
Sweden
www.boklok.com

Cartwright Pickard Architects
16 Regent's Wharf
London N1 9RL England
tel. +44 207 837 7023

Choi-Campagna Design
Sheila Choi & Adam Campagna
Choi-Campagna
515 Canal Street, Suite 1C
New York, NY 10013
tel. 212.226.8845
choicampagna@aol.com

Collins and Turner Architects
Studio 15, 151 Foveaux Street
Surry Hills NSW 2010 Australia
tel. 61 02 9356 3217
www.collinsandturner.com

Pierre d'Avoine Architects
6A Orde Hall Street
London WC1N 3JW England
tel. +44 20 7242 2124
mail@davoine.net

First Penthouse
The Loft, Albert Court
Prince Consort Road
London SW7 2BE
United Kingdom
tel. +44(0) 20 7584 9894
www.firstpenthouse.co.uk

FORM
1813–17 Lincoln Boulevard
Venice, CA 90291
tel. 310.821.2629
www.glform.com

Gláma Kim Arkitektar
Laugavegi 164 ehf
105 Reykjavik, Iceland
tel. +354 530 8106
www.glamakim.is

Heikkinen-Komonen Architects
Kristianinkatu 11–13
00170 Helsinki, Finland
tel. +358 9 751 02 111
www.heikkinen-komonen.fi

David Hertz
Syndesis, Inc.
2908 Colorado Avenue
Santa Monica, CA 90404
tel. 310.829.9932
www.syndesisinc.com

KFN Systems
www.kaufmannkaufmann.com

Johannes Kaufmann Architektur
Sägerstrasse 4
6850 Dornbirn, Austria
tel. +43 (0) 5572 23 690
www.jkarch.at

Oskar Leo Kaufmann
Ziviltechniker Gesmbh
Steinebach 3
6850 Dornbirn, Austria
tel. +43 5572 39 49 69
www.olk.cc

Craig Konyk
Konyk Architecture
61 Pearl Street, #509
Brooklyn, NY 11201
tel. 718.852.5381
www.konyk.net

Krill Architecture
Urban Planning and Research
Vierhavensstraat 1–7
3029 BB Rotterdam
The Netherlands
tel. +31 10 477 9247
www.krill.nl

Anders Landström
Landström Arkitekter
Alsnögatan 12
116 41 Stockholm, Sweden
tel. +46 08 679 90 60
www.landstrom.se

Oosterhuis.nl
Essenburgsingel 94c
3022 EG Rotterdam
The Netherlands
tel. +31 10 244 7039
www.oosterhuis.nl/variomatic/

Open Office
330 West 38th Street
New York, NY 10018
tel. 212.931.6288
www.open-office.net

Piercy Conner Architects
Cairo Studios
4–6 Nile Street
London N1 7RF England
tel. +44 207 4909494
www.piercyconner.co.uk

Rocio Romero
Rocio Romero Design
4942 West Pine St. #3e
Saint Louis, Mo 63108
tel:314-367-0182
www.rocioromero.com

Thomas Sandell
Sandell Sandberg
Riddargatan 17 D 11
SE-114 57 Stockholm, Sweden
tel. +46 8506 217 00
www.sandellsandberg.se

Jennifer Siegal
Office of Mobile Design
939 Indiana Avenue
Los Angeles, CA 90291
tel. 310.399.5560
www.designmobile.com

Wickham van Eyck Architects
382–386 Edgeware Road
London W2 1EB England
tel. +44(0) 20 7402 0669
Entrepotdok 23-24
1018 AD Amsterdam
The Netherlands
tel. +31 20 6230 947
www.wickhamvaneyck.com

Richard Wintersole, AIA
649 Quail Ridge Road
Aledo, TX 76008
tel. 817.441.9783

INDEX